ARKANA

Working on Yourself Alone

A key figure in the revolutionary field of dream and body work, conflict resolution and of psychological interventions in psychiatry, Arnold Mindell is the author of *Dreambody*, *Working with the Dreaming Body*, *River's Way*, *The Dreambody in Relationships*, *City Shadows* and *The Year 1* (all published by Arkana), and *Coma, Door of Awakening*. He is an analyst in private practice, Founder of the Center for Process-oriented Psychology, Portland and Zurich, and analyst and teacher both at this society and at the Jung Institute, Zurich. He has been a resident teacher at Esalen Institute, Big Sur, California.

ARNOLD MINDELL

Working on Yourself Alone

Inner Dreambody Work

ARKANA

ARKANA

Published by the Penguin Group
27 Wrights Lane, London W8 5TZ, England
Viking Penguin Inc., 40 West 23rd Street, New York, New York 10010, USA
Penguin Books Australia Ltd, Ringwood, Victoria, Australia
Penguin Books Canada Ltd, 2801 John Street, Markham, Ontario, Canada L3R 1B4
Penguin Books (NZ) Ltd, 182–190 Wairau Road, Auckland 10, New Zealand

Penguin Books Ltd, Registered Offices: Harmondsworth, Middlesex, England

First published 1990
10 9 8 7 6 5 4 3 2 1

Made and printed in Great Britain by
Richard Clay Ltd, Bungay, Suffolk

Filmset in 10.5 pt Ehrhardt

CONTENTS

LIST OF ILLUSTRATIONS

Acknowledgements

I would especially like to thank Barbara Croci for having helped me in every imaginable way during the experimental phase of my meditation work and for having aided me in developing the Working on Yourself Alone seminar series from which some aspects of this book have been taken. Barbara taught me hatha yoga and together we began to transform the ancient spiritual practice into a process-oriented meditation procedure.

I am also greatly indebted to Carl Mindell for having fired me up about meditation years ago, for having introduced me to Muktananda's siddha yoga and to vipasyana meditation, and for his many helpful references to other writers in the field.

I am also greatly indebted to the Center for Process-oriented Psychology of Zurich and Portland and allied groups in Denver, Seattle, Boston and Santa Cruz who have tested the ideas in this book in experimental seminars. Jan Dworkin, Reinhard Hauser, Amy Kaplan, Dawn Menken, Debbie Schüpbach, Suzanne Springs and Madeleine Ziegler gave me many valuable additions and corrections. Many thanks to Katherine Ziegler for her helpful comments and suggestions, and especially to Julie Diamond for her editorial assistance.

I am very thankful to Stephan Bodian of the *Yoga Journal* for having noticed, at the last moment, a few of the more obvious errors I made in speaking about eastern meditation procedures. Amy Kaplan strongly encouraged me to bring this work to conclusion and to write Chapter 11.

For permission to reproduce the illustrations in this book grateful acknowledgement is made to the following:

Acknowledgements

1 courtesy of the Royal Ontario Museum, Toronto; *2* courtesy of HOA-QUI Edition et Agence d'Illustration Photographique; *3, 4a, 4b and 4c* the Estate of C. G. Jung, c/o Niedieck Linder AG, Zurich; *5a, 5b and 6*, from B. K. S. Iyengar, *Light on Yoga*, Unwin Hyman; *7–13* Arlette Loquin; *14* Detroit Institute of Arts, gift of Mr and Mrs Bert L. Smokler and Mr and Mrs Lawrence A. Fleischman; *15* Arnold Mindell; *16* courtesy of the Kungliga Biblioteket, Stockholm; *17* courtesy of the Ajit Mookerji Collection, New Delhi; *18*, from H. Storm, *Seven Arrows*, Harper & Row Publishers, Inc., New York.

PREFACE

This book is, I believe, part of a new, wide-spectrum approach in psychology and meditation to working alone on dreams, body feelings, creative movement and relationships. *Working on Yourself Alone* is meant to be a self-contained introductory and training manual on inner work on oneself using process-oriented psychology without the help of a therapist. It is meant for anyone interested in meditation and psychotherapy.

The present meditation study develops the introverted aspect of what I originally called 'dreambodywork'. In *Dreambody* (1984) I present the discovery that body experiences are somatic maps of dreams; *Working with the Dreaming Body* (1985) demonstrates the information and channel structures of process work. *River's Way* (1986) outlines its philosophical foundations. *The Dreambody in Relationships* (1987) applies dreambody language to family work, and *City Shadows* approaches extreme and psychotic states. Now, *Working on Yourself Alone* shows how information, channel awareness and process theory create a useful self-help technique.

This book is the result of two five-day sittings. The first took place during the summer of 1981 while I was mountaineering near the Col de la Croix pass in Switzerland and the second in the early fall of 1984 while I was relaxing on the Oregon coast in the United States. These two extended meditations produced, quite unexpectedly, the book you now have in your hands.

It is only now, seven years after having first started the book, that I feel sufficiently confident to share it with you. I have thoroughly tested and improved upon it with the help of hundreds of students of inner work and am convinced of its potential usefulness for different kinds of people in every imaginable state. It is intended for anyone interested in unravelling the mysteries of dreams, body experiences, relationships and synchronicities. The first three chapters focus upon the basic and sometimes hidden assumptions of current meditation procedures. The second part of the work presents my own meditation on developing the first steps of process-oriented meditation. Part I is meant to challenge the reader's mind, while Part II is offered as an aid to working alone on oneself. Part III, World Work, applies inner work to relationships and global processes.

The goal of this book is to create a common ground supporting both eastern and western practices through the use of information and process concepts. It attempts to integrate eastern meditation, western body-oriented psychotherapies, analytical psychologies and information theory. It might be a guide, for both novices and advanced students, to using meditation for internal exploration and also for working with others.

After much indecision, I have left the work largely in its original form, namely as a process-oriented meditation, so that it clearly communicates the most important ideas. Leaving it primarily in the form of a meditation has the advantage of appealing to the reader interested in experiencing the work at the same time as reading it.

I would like to apologize for any difficulties arising from the mixture of linear and meditative writing styles and I invite the reader to join me in an adventure which I could not undertake in any other way. The reader searching for logical consistency, implications, and connections to other systems will be able, I hope, to find some answers in the first part of the work and in Chapter 12, Questions.

The questions and answers about process-oriented meditation in Chapter 12 are included not only for information but also to aid research. I am interested in including the reader in the present study. If you have questions which are not addressed here, I invite you to share them with me. I will include them in possible future editions in the hope that this work becomes a collective research project on meditation.

Arnold Mindell
Avers, 1987

PART I
Hidden Assumptions

Chapter 1

MEDITATION PROBLEMS

EASTERN AND WESTERN WAYS

Though many similarities exist between western psychotherapy and eastern meditation procedures, there is no doubt that, generally speaking, western psychotherapy is more extraverted than the eastern approaches to the individual, and thus frequently conflicts with the beliefs and goals of eastern meditation procedures.

There is an interesting story illustrating the conflict between eastern and western psychology. This incident took place on western soil when Ram Dass, one of the leading American proponents of eastern thought, met Fritz Perls, one of the most popular psychotherapists of our time. They apparently met for the first time on a radio show and, according to Ram Dass, his reaction to Perls was to turn inward and become silent; Perls immediately reproached him for avoiding confrontation and behaving in such a detached fashion.[1]

I hope the reader will excuse this polarization of these two men as representatives of opposing worlds. But I would like to suggest that Ram Dass represented, at least at that time, the attempt to introvert, focus internally and empty the mind of inner voices. Perls represented the opposite attitude, the one which proposes that 'going internal' avoids life and its difficulties. The story portrays the one-sidedness of both the introverted meditative attitude towards life and the extraverted encounter method of dealing with relationship conflicts.

EXTRAVERTED FOCUS

The extraverted focus of western psychotherapy, as represented by Perls in the story told by Ram Dass, has enabled us to develop powerful ways of interacting with clients and relationships. Yet the exclusiveness of this focus leaves therapists relatively inexperienced in working with themselves. I have found from supervising and training therapists from various schools that certain professional inadequacies can be traced to insufficient experience of working internally. This lack of inner experience

1 cuts us off from an empathetic understanding of introverted processes such as silence, non-verbal communication, withdrawn states, catatonia and comatose conditions[2]
2 makes us fear, neglect and inhibit our own and our clients' internal experiences when these try to surface
3 makes it difficult for us to deal with negative transference situations, and so forces the work out of our given psychological programme
4 makes us depend excessively upon colleagues, police and hospitals
5 tends to make clients overly dependent upon us since little effort is made to teach them how to work alone.

FRAGMENTATION IN WESTERN PROCEDURES

Western psychology today consists of hundreds of different schools and approaches which, for the most part, have little connection to one another. Body work and massage are still largely separate from verbal psychotherapies, just as family work lacks the introverted methods of dream work and body work. We know something about doing therapy with one another but very little about how to do it alone.

C. G. Jung's 'active imagination', a western method for working alone on visual material, is a potent form of introverted work with dreams and visions. The student confronts the dream figures alone and on paper, just as in the Gestalt 'hot seat' method the client uses a therapist and an empty chair (Perls 1969). The extended version of active imagination includes working with paints or sand trays (Kalf 1981). Mary Whitehouse's 'Authentic Movement' extends active imagination by integrating it with dance (Whitehouse 1979). The interrelationship between dreams, body work, active imagination and authentic dance remains a research area in meditation practice.

Another very useful method of inner work is recommended by Charles Tart (1987) in *Waking Up*. He has succeeded here in combining Gurdjieff's idea that we are spiritually sleeping with sensory grounded meditation exercises to produce one of the best practical meditation guides to date.

EASTERN PRACTICES

Like western instructors, many Buddhist teachers are, in principle, open to all experiences, techniques and religions, but in practice they tend to stress an inner focus which represses fantasies, spontaneous thoughts or ideas, and emotional affects. As a result, meditators are often bothered by unavoidable 'disturbances' which they are taught to tolerate. Many meditators have undoubtedly felt like Charles Tart at one time or another:

> I have practiced various forms of meditation off and on for many years, but have never been very successful at it. I sometimes half-jokingly (and half-sadly) describe myself as an expert on the difficulties of meditation as a result of so much experience of my mind wandering off instead of focusing! In spite of my intellectual knowledge of the importance of meditation practice, some confusion as to just what to do, and the consequent lack of results sapped my motivations, so I have not regularly practiced formal meditation for years.
>
> (Tart 1986)

It seems to me that Tart at this point was suffering from the covert assumption of many meditation procedures that the distracting experiences should not be there. Let us look more closely at some of the eastern procedures and their assumptions.

Vipasyana and Samatha

Tart opens new territory when he speaks of Shinzen Young's excellent review of meditation (Young 1986), which points to the two cornerstones of eastern meditation, samatha, calming the body and mind, and vipasyana, heightening clarity and awareness. These cornerstones are found in Theravada, Tantra and Zen, and are also reflected in Christian contemplative practice.

Various methods can be used to achieve samatha: relaxed sitting, visualizing or breathing. Chanting is also a commonly used centring technique in China, Japan, Korea, Vietnam and in Eastern Orthodox Christianity. According to these ancient practices, samatha without vipasyana is trance without awareness. On the other hand, vipasyana without samatha is a kind of psychic 'tripping'.

The Stream of Nobles

There are various goals in meditation. Sustained focus on what happens within and without produces a breakthrough experience of freedom which the scholastic Buddhists call 'entering the stream of nobles'. This means breaking off an identification with only one state and giving way to a detached contact with inner states and processes.

Kensho

The Rinzai school speaks of kensho, or seeing one's nature. Young equates such enlightenment with satori, or catching on. Kensho and satori describe the 'aha' experience of realizing who you are and what is essential to life. It is discovering that you are, surprisingly enough, the figures you dream about.

The Japanese Soto Zen school stresses simple meditation. Its goal is to be who you are and to live your Buddha nature, which means, in psychological terms, something like knowing and being congruently who you are in any given moment.

SIMILARITIES AND DIFFERENCES

We will find process-oriented meditation to be both different from and, in many ways, similar to these meditation procedures. Process work is like vipasyana in its stress on awareness. Process-oriented meditation, however, does not necessarily begin with samatha, that is, with relieving tension through a calming method, because tensions and other 'distractions' are part of the mercurial process we are interested in. In fact, we will see that when tensions are worked with, they can become a rapid path to satori.

Process work has much in common with Soto Zen in that the method of working *is* the goal. Preference is not given to any particular state, either stressful or peaceful, but to the ability to live completely in the moment, in every way possible.

THE RELATIONSHIP CHANNEL

Many spiritual eastern traditions ritualize or programme personal relationships and neglect problems in communication. Avoiding relationship processes has the advantage of heightening introverted experience, but repressing affects in relationships never really succeeds; it tends only to create more outer conflicts, since the avoided emotions come up in another way.

MIND STUFF

I have often wondered why so many teachers seem to look down on everyday emotions and so-called 'mind stuff', the bulk of mental life. Some teachers count breaths, concentrate rigorously on given objects, note the pulse or repeat a mantra to gain control over the senses. Yet blocking certain sense perceptions in favour of others only hoodwinks the conscious mind. Sensory signals cannot be destroyed by focusing on something else; they are merely repressed. If they are not dealt with directly, they often sidetrack the meditation and make it necessary to spend months or years reaching a state which could have taken minutes if the disturbing thoughts such as greed and jealousy had been processed consciously.

Many new age practices send out conflicting messages about greed, jealousy, and hatred, the 'lower human drives'. Some teachers advise dealing neutrally with these drives: 'Let them go through you while noting them.' Others teach that one should get beyond these lower drives, and realize love and compassion for all sentient beings. Other approaches prescribe certain moral precepts to maintain purity of body, speech and mind, which are difficult to follow.[3]

One reason why conflicting messages often associated with eastern practices are so widely accepted by western meditators is that there is no east or west when it comes to personal problems. Everyone wants to get beyond pain, everyone fears egotism and compulsion, and everyone desires peace from ambition. Yet I have often seen that the greatest changes occur when the troublesome parts of the personality are allowed to express themselves, truly to unfold with the appreciation of consciousness.

If you are greedy or ambitious, try consciously identifying with these drives. Stand behind them and help them to unfold their messages. You need not try to do away with them, for they begin to change as soon as their messages are expressed and appreciated.

ENLIGHTENMENT OR NEW AGE INFLATION?

Eastern and western psychology both concede that change is only temporary; only process itself is permanent. Thus, any attempt to reach or produce a state of mind such as that in the highest stage of awareness is bound to have only temporary success.

One state of mind that people often aspire to is loving compassion towards others. When this goal is reached as a spontaneous occurrence, and not as a programme organized by the ego, it is a very meaningful and powerful way to be in the world. For most people, however, loving compassion tends to be an inflexible state, a goal to be reached. Such people are frequently naïve about themselves and often reveal hidden prejudices and contempt towards others.

Thus, misinterpreting eastern philosophy can lead to an inflated view of oneself. Meditators striving for enlightenment often view others as 'lower', 'stuck in the elemental passions', or as having a 'primitive mind'. This state of affairs mirrors a similar trap in western psychology. The analyst and his or her client tend to act 'whole', 'together', or 'cool', even when they are not!

THE DANGERS OF RELAXATION

Total relaxation and letting go of tension-creating thoughts may be unhealthy. Any method, even massage, can be dangerous if used to relax, unless it is followed by an exact, differentiated processing of what the original tensions were. There are two reasons for this.

First, years of body work with ill people have shown that a previous history of tension repression was frequently present before the onset of cancer. Tension, like any other process, cannot be put away by magic, though it can be removed from awareness for short periods of time. Repressed or relaxed tension does not disappear; it seems to become less tractable to consciousness. One of the possible courses for repressed processes like tension is to create intractable symptoms and diseases such as cancer.

Second, I wonder if letting tension go, or 'shaking it out', as is customary in some meditation, body work and massage procedures, is good ecology for the rest of us living in this universe. Around the world people are becoming aware of the dangers of simply throwing waste down the drain. Just as the water system of the earth becomes clogged and disturbed, so throwing tension into the wind may clog up the spiritual system of the planet, the place the rest of us drink from when we are thirsty. If the globe is a system or field, we cannot throw something *out*; we can only put it back *into* the system. We should consider the possibility that information is not destroyed, but thrown into the global information float, Jung's collective unconscious; it then becomes a cloud of trouble picked up by someone else in the field.

I think it is safer to process psychic wastes. Why simply programme your mind to 'relax', or to 'replace your old thoughts with new images' (Adair 1984)? Though such procedures are simple to use, they may have the disadvantage of creating individual illness or disturbing the psychic ecology of our planet. They do not seem to appreciate that each individual meditation process has its own special, innate method for working out problems. In my opinion, our job should be to discover this individual method.

SUMMARY

Some of the characteristics of eastern and western inner work methods may be summed up as follows:

1 Western psychology's extraverted focus on clinical work and personal interactions inhibits our interest in understanding of how to work alone, without a therapist.

2 Eastern methods oriented towards reaching a detached state of mind can achieve this without rigid meditation procedures which programme awareness to focus upon a specific object, sentence or body experience.

3 Meditation's tendency to avoid emotional interactions between people induces unnecessary strain in relationships through the repression of greed, jealousy and egotism.

4 Any psychology which represses body tension and inner difficulties only makes them less accessible to awareness. It is possible that they enter into the collective psychological field or reappear in the individual's cellular processes which may be inaccessible to awareness.

5 Most meditation procedures, not including t'ai chi or Authentic Movement, neglect creative and spontaneous movement and emotion. No procedure I am familiar with recommends people to discover or create movement. Vipasyana and Zen either inhibit spontaneous movement or programme specific kinds of movement.

6 Many meditation procedures annihilate ordinary, everyday concerns and produce altered states of consciousness, not just because of the mind-expanding nature of altered states, but because the procedures themselves are unable to deal with everyday problems in any other way.

RETHINKING MEDITATION

Can we develop an inner work which will enable us to discover our own innate meditation procedure and which will satisfy the needs met by existing eastern and western approaches? The difficulties in western psychology and eastern meditation rituals may imply that the goals and belief systems which organize them are insufficient to deal with the problems arising from their use. Perhaps we

11

should start from the beginning and develop a new system because the problems outlined above cannot be solved by merely adding more techniques to existing methods.

Chapter 2

PARADIGM SHIFTS IN MEDITATION

A new paradigm in meditation should fulfil both the old and new goals, but the way in which these are met will be different. Typical modern and ancient aims in development are: following the unconscious (as in analytical psychology), increasing and freeing energy (as in acupressure and other body work systems), divining the Tao (as in the *I Ching*), becoming a warrior (as in Castaneda and Trungpa), detaching from illusion (as in Buddhism), and entering the stream (as in vipasyana meditation).[1] The process paradigm incorporates these goals by working on dreams and body phenomena, following the stream of energy in the dreambody, enabling meditators to understand or even guess what hexagram they will get from the *I Ching*, disciplining the warrior in 'seeing', actualizing the 'fair observer' of the Buddhist meditator, and developing the fluidity of a vipasyana meditator.

GOALS ARE PROCESSES

A fascinating characteristic of meditation goals is that they are influenced by our images of the ideal, developed human being, and these images themselves change as we grow. Can we find a meditation procedure which will meet our immediate goals and also be able to change as our goals change? If I begin process-oriented meditation, will I be able to find my beloved Zen goals today, for example, and then tomorrow fulfil my need to understand a dream or relationship problem? Will I be able actually to solve everyday problems or resolve illnesses?

Process-oriented concepts should

1 include other meditation procedures
2 enable one to follow the automatic and individual process of changing goals as one develops
3 have already proven useful in revealing the meaning and alleviating the pain of psychosomatic symptoms
4 enable one to discover various meditation procedures within oneself. Hatha yoga, creative movement and dance, relationship work, vision quests, visualizations and internal dialoguing occur naturally in meditation, even when one has not previously studied them
5 lend themselves readily to criticism and investigation.

IS BEING HUMAN WRONG?

One of the fundamental and sometimes unconscious tenets found in many psychologies and meditation procedures is that the human being is undisciplined, unaware, loveless, filled with greed, jealousy and egotism, dangerous and somehow wrong. Behind these tenets lies the implicit belief that people are not right the way they are.

Most of us believe this. We think that we are not in order, that the world is a mess and cannot be changed. We are plagued by strange dreams, internal voices, body symptoms, relationship problems, pollution, poisoned food and aggressive neighbours. These beliefs lead us to use our rational intellect to understand our dreams, analyse the voices away, meditate on mantras, develop medicine to overcome our symptoms, programme our affects into acceptable channels of communication, and create armies to protect us from one another. Our beliefs push us to war and we sometimes, though only momentarily, win a battle against our natures. Believing things are 'wrong' makes us think causally; it divides the world into problems and solutions. This old paradigm has helped us prolong our life by making psychological and chemical warfare against symptoms and disturbing inner parts.

But the warlike belief that our natures are wrong overlooks the potential purpose behind events. I am not ill simply because I have not taken enough vitamins or meditated enough or because of my genetic inheritance. It could be that my problems represent a part of me which I do not yet know about.

A second problem with causal thinking is that it makes us dislike the world when it does not meet our expectations. If we cannot solve a problem, we turn against it. Aggressive nations and insane despots do not meet my expectations for world peace. I would like to change them, but cannot. If I am not careful, I will declare 'war' on them, try to put them down or in insane asylums. We have to learn how to use insanity and aggression in a more useful form.

ALL EVENTS ARE POTENTIALLY USEFUL

We need to add a new dimension to our belief about being human. This new dimension sounds like an ancient one which states: 'The world is perfect the way it is.' Even though I do not feel the world is really perfect the way it is I have discovered great enrichment from seemingly adverse events. An important and possibly new dimension in meditation would be to accept and process all events, including anger, jealousy and greed, in order to reveal their life-giving potential. Instead of trying to change our natures to fit our preconceptions of harmony or peace, we could seek to find the purpose behind events. Perhaps they are the seeds of just what we need.

My questions are: How can I make use of all my perceptions for my own benefit and for the rest of the world? Who is observing? Who in me wants to get rid of problems?

COMPASSION

Now let's begin to discuss process concepts. Rejecting parts of ourselves cannot really succeed for they cannot simply be eradicated. A more compassionate inner attitude would be to assume that bad moods, aches and pains, negative thoughts etc. are at least potentially useful.

Compassion is a crucial element of process work because it lovingly tolerates and accepts potential growth in ourselves. 'Loving kindness' and other types of spiritual feelings for others thus transform in process work into accepting and processing all of those events which reach our awareness. This means appreciating that all of our parts and relationship interactions can potentially evolve into personal growth. There are no 'good' or 'bad' people: all of us are parts of a whole requiring awareness and interaction.

Therefore, at the centre of process work will be a compassionate awareness of our own perceptions. Every psychological and meditation intervention has a governing philosophy behind it and, as far as I am aware, this paradigm in process work is compassion. Philosophy implies that nature is not bad; it is whatever it is. People are neither nice nor nasty, your body feels well or is sick, you have fine or awful dreams, you have critical or loving voices in your ears, you make awkward or beautiful movements, you are happy or depressed, the world acts as if it were at your feet or it turns against you. Whatever happens is the awareness process, the basic material of the meditation.

ALCHEMY AND AMPLIFICATION

Compassion alone is not enough; we also need a 'cooking' method, so to speak. An alchemist would say that the awareness process is the *prima materia*, the magical stuff about to be cooked, the substance which will transform. The basic material is *process*: *signals undergoing change*. To continue the alchemical metaphor, the alchemist puts process (signals) into the meditation pot (focus) and cooks (amplifies) them to completion. Whatever is happening, whatever the alchemist perceives, she cooks, be it pleasant, awful, confusing or weird. She puts her feelings and opinions about the processes into the pot, too, and cooks it all together; in time she hopes the mixture turns to gold.

The Alchemist's Gold

And what is this gold? The alchemist's beginning goals will be like yours or mine: freedom from trouble, hope for nirvana, enlightenment, love, immortality or spontaneity. But what you actually receive may be something you were not even aware of missing, something so precious and vital that you might even forget your original goals.

The alchemist's gold is greater contact with experience of, and sometimes even insight into, her own and others' nature. This gold comes in the exact form she needs. The alchemist may get increased warmth, love and flexibility, increased sense of warriorship or toughness, freedom from symptoms, or simply an end to exhaustion. Whatever finally occurs will be a process connecting her to the core of events.

PROCESS AND SIGNALS

The starting-point is the process, the basic stuff which we shall cook. Take this process, plus your feelings about it, put them in a pot, and you are ready to begin. This is just what alchemy and Taoism have been teaching for thousands of years. Perhaps one of the reasons why alchemy, Taoism, eastern rituals and many western psychologies are difficult to use is because they have not defined exactly what the process or its signals are, so let us try to define it here.

Process is information which comes to you in specific ways or channels such as seeing, hearing, moving, feeling, relationships, and the world.

For example, right now I am sitting on the Oregon coast. I see myself (visual channel) in a beach hut and hear and see the sea in front of me. So I could cook these perceptions by amplifying my seeing and hearing. The process changes the signals which I see and hear, and I find myself looking down at my typewriter, hearing a giant in the sea about 200 feet in front of me. I try to listen, but feel the heat of the last rays of the summer sun on my back – proprioceptively with my body – as the sun sinks into the water's horizon. I notice the movements in my hand and the stillness of my posture. Suddenly I am aware of a feeling of openness resulting from a recent discussion I had with Barbara Croci about writing. I now imagine that I am writing not only to a few people but to the world at large. Is it a spirit from the sea who writes? As I amplify him, cook him, I realize that it is not yet time to stop writing.

YOUR THREE PERSONALITIES

Let me ask you a question. Do you know what is happening to you when you are not meditating, when you are not picking up your perceptions? What are you doing most of the time?

If you cannot answer this question, it probably indicates that whatever you do most of the time must be unconscious, i.e. outside your awareness. You might say that when you are not meditating, you are just living your life: you get up, you eat and sleep, you work, care for yourself, provide for your family and others. But then I would have to ask, 'Who is it that does these things? Is this the totality of yourself?' You will probably answer, 'No.' You know this is not the totality of yourself because sometimes a little something in you has thoughts about what you are doing.

You, or something in you, is thinking about you; you are 'meta'-thinking, that is, thinking about your thinking. Such relativity means that you either have to be in two places at once or else you have to be two people at the same time; or rather, three. You are the one doing something, the one reacting to this doing, that is, being happy or unhappy about your work, and you are also the observer who perceives the interaction of the doer and reactor.

PRIMARY AND SECONDARY PROCESSES

In process theory, we speak of a primary process with which you identify yourself most of the time. This primary process is the part you call 'I', the part which you see 'doing' your life, playing certain roles, working and performing duties.

Then there are secondary considerations and disturbances which are normally not united with, i.e. congruent with, your doings. A secondary process reacts to and makes it difficult to pay attention to what you are doing; it is the source of body problems and relationship trouble. *The secondary process is what the meditator usually calls a distraction.* A secondary process may appear in the world as an accident thwarting your intent or as a dream awakening you out of your sleep. The secondary you is not always in agreement with the primary you.

THE METACOMMUNICATOR

And finally there is a sort of 'fair observer', a metacommunicator who, when she or he is awake, can observe both the primary and secondary processes as if from above, on the mountain top, and is able to talk about these insights and perceptions.

UP OR DOWN WITH THE EGO?

What happens to the ego process in theory?

Eastern and western teachers define the ego differently because they base their observations upon different paradigms. Many western psychologists maintain that your ego should be developed and defended. Most eastern teachers, however, advise getting rid of it; there is no ego, they say, there is only the so-called 'fair witness'. Both definitions understand the ego as a static state, which, of course, it rarely is. Process-oriented thinking gets around this problem by defining the ego as one of our possible observers. *The ego is, to begin with at least, the 'I' which identifies itself with the doings of the world.*

The ego is born as the twin of the primary process. Thus, in the beginning, it is one-sided like the primary process, which irritates the eastern meditator. This is why she wants to get rid of the ego. She actually wants to wake the ego up, stop its identification with everyday concerns, detach it from them, look at them, and notice the secondary processes as well. The meditator hopes to transform the ego from a one-sided one who looks at the primary process into a fair observer.

During meditation, the 'I', the ego as defined by western psychology, runs into trouble because it meets with secondary processes which are at odds with the primary ones it has identified with until now. For example, let us say that, at first, the ego identified itself as a nice person. Now, it discovers mean figures in the secondary process, i.e. in dreams, visions, projections, etc., which cause it conflict. This conflict creates tension, and a constant flipping of the 'I', identifying one moment with the primary process and the next moment with the secondary ones.

FLIPPING AND DETACHMENT

Much to the chagrin of our environment which knew us once as predictable and nice people, we now 'flip' into the mean guy at certain times as we grow and change. Through the processes of nature, the help of psychotherapy or the aid of meditation teachers, the ego, which had been at first one process and then the other, detaches itself from both and becomes a 'fair observer', or metacommunicator and observes both parts of itself in a neutral fashion.

The classical therapist speaks to the metacommunicator, without identifying it as such, when making interpretations about the other parts. In fact, verbal therapies depend on the metacommunicator. This is why most western psychologies want to build up and strengthen the ego, the primary process; it must grow to the point where it can observe itself and the secondary process.

Eastern teachings reach the same goal from a different direction. Through meditation the ego loosens its tie to the primary process, eventually transforming into a metacommunicator. The theoretical differences between the two schools occur because the east stresses the transience of all things while the west focuses on the importance of this world.

Thus, they differ about what the ego is or should be. Both use the term, but associate it with different stationary states, either with a primary 'I' or a state detached from both primary and secondary processes. A process-oriented paradigm uses yet another method of viewing the ego. In process terms, it is one state or stage in the development of the metacommunicator, the fair observer.

THE PRIMARY PROCESS

I regret having to use the new terms 'primary and secondary processes', but there seems to be no way out. I use the word 'primary process' instead of its close approximate, 'consciousness', because the primary process is usually compulsive, whereas consciousness implies awareness and the possibility of control.

In meditation we can observe that our normal behaviour is compulsive; the thoughts organizing our 'normality' are outside our control! We do the doings of the world as if unknowingly programmed to do them. This doing is maya! The doer is a dream figure, one with which we are normally identified. We may want to change our behaviour but will find ourselves doing the same old things over and over again. This is why eastern meditators attempt to stop the primary process or the ego normally associated with it.

They want to stop the world and free themselves from its cycling, from the rigid ego.

For example, while I am on vacation here on the Oregon coast, I frequently get up in the morning, eat breakfast and talk to Barbara, even if I am not congruently involved in these actions. Thus, much of my eating and talking is a primary process. It keeps my world going. My secondary process may have no interest in talking or eating. My metacommunicator is the one writing about and observing these activities; he is the me who does not identify with either process but giggles at them both, trying to get the primary one to open up to the secondary one.

On Recommending Meditation

I cannot recommend meditation to someone as long as she is identified with and content with her primary process, and as long as there is no secondary one strong enough to conflict with it. Such a person is reasonably congruent and content. She is happy the way she is and needs nothing else. Some of the greatest people are those who, with the brute strength of their primary process and the miraculousness of their human nature, overcome personal problems, struggle through impasses, become individuals, go against the judgement of their neighbours in becoming themselves, and do all of this without recognition and without ever meditating. The need to meditate arises when our primary identification, our normal way of living, no longer works well. Meditation arises spontaneously when our inner life can no longer remain still, when it begins to rumble and dream, revolt and excite us to awake.

Chapter 3

CHANNELS AND MEDITATION RITUALS

Our sensory channels can be used to reorganize known meditation procedures without reference to their philosophical base. In addition, the use of channels is a powerful tool in dealing with difficult aspects of meditation. As an introduction, let us consider the following channels and the different meditation procedures based on them:

1 Body feeling or proprioception: hatha yoga, zen breath counting, massage, autogenic training, relaxation techniques, biofeedback
2 Visualization: one-pointed observation, yantra meditation, dream work
3 Hearing: drumming, mantra, prayer meditation, internal dialoguing
4 Movement or kinaesthesis: T'ai chi, Sufi dancing, authentic movement
5 Relationships: Tantra, Taoist alchemy, siddha yoga
6 World phenomena: American Indian vision quest.

In Chapter 4 I will explain briefly the different techniques found in each of the channels. A thorough investigation of each of the meditation procedures would be a work unto itself.

CHANNEL OCCUPATION AND ALTERED STATES

Most meditation procedures attract us and affect our behaviour

23

through altering our states of awareness. An altered state occurs when we focus upon the sensory perceptions which we do not consciously use. Let me explain altered states and their relationship to channels.

We use all of the above channels (and more) all of the time. Yet we only use some to identify ourselves. The ones we frequently and consciously use are 'occupied' by our awareness. If we do not use them with intent, they are 'unoccupied' by our conscious awareness. Our unconscious awareness may still use them, but we simply do not pay attention to them. If a channel, such as visualization, is 'occupied', then focusing on it gives you the feeling of familiarity. If a channel is unused or 'unoccupied', then focusing on it gives you a weird, dreamlike, or 'far-out' feeling.

One of the least developed channels in most of us is body feeling or proprioception. Proprioception is usually unoccupied by our normal focus. This means that we do not pay attention to our body temperature, its pressures and its tensions. Focusing on an unoccupied channel such as proprioception creates an altered state; it 'stops the world', for intentionally feeling the world is more foreign to us than seeing it.

Proprioception

Any ritual or meditation procedure which recommends that you focus upon proprioceptive experiences, such as the feeling of your breath, your muscles or heartbeat, automatically produces an altered state. Your ordinary sense of the world is stopped by using an unoccupied channel, regardless of the religious or philosophical beliefs which accompany such focus.

Rituals like Zen meditation where the practitioner focuses upon breathing sensations, or hatha yoga where the student notes the limitations of his musculature during the body postures called asanas, give us access to proprioceptive experiences and a rest from our normal world (Suzuki 1970; Iyengar 1968).

Autogenic training reprogrammes awareness to proprioception by focusing on tension and temperatures in different parts of the body. This relaxes the musculature creating our primary drives and diverts focus from our main channels to allow an experience of what has hitherto been unknown territory (Schultz and Luthe 1955).

Massage also awakens proprioception through increasing awareness of body parts which we normally cannot touch. Altered states of consciousness are induced through massage by switching the recipient out of his normal channels and raising proprioception through touching, and stretching and relaxing the musculature.

VISUALIZATION

Rituals which focus the vision upon geometrical designs such as yantras or mandalas produce peace and centredness by programming sight upon a harmonious structure rather than letting the vision focus upon anything which comes its way (Khanna 1979). Altered states are created, not by switching channels but by blocking a main channel and filling it with new information (see illustration 1).

Visualization can also produce an altered state if the occupied focus was a proprioception such as pain. Someone in a great deal of pain would find focusing on a candle or visualizing a point of light a very powerful way of reducing the pain. The symptoms causing the pain have not actually diminished; rather, one's awareness has switched from proprioception to visualization. Have you ever noticed that when you sit in the dentist's chair, you block the pain in your mouth by pinching your fingers together or looking at one point on the ceiling? This is an unconscious attempt to switch channels and change the object of your proprioception.

The popularity of many meditation rituals stems partly from

1 A mandala as visual meditation

2 Drumming as auditory meditation

the need that people have for mind-affecting drugs, watching television or visiting friends. People have an unconscious need to switch channels, to break free of the primary process and pain, and to transform life. Channel-changing methods presented later in this work will aid the reader in working with pain so that it can be transmuted instead of obliterated.

Auditory Rituals

Drumming, loud music or even television commercials can fill our auditory channel, and block normal, internal dialogue to induce an altered state of consciousness (Wosien 1972, and see illustration 2). Reciting mantras, repeating a given prayer, singing or humming have the same effect (ibid.). Auditory signals induce trance

27

states in two ways. They either blot out the ordinary internal dialogues or switch the focus into proprioception, since rhythm and music can also be felt physically, not just heard. We all know that we can feel singing through the vibrations in our lungs, back, throat and head.

I recently met a shaman whose central healing method was to bite or lightly thrash the suffering person (thereby amplifying his proprioception) until he found his song. The interaction between proprioception and music happens, in this case, through feeling one's pain acutely and translating it into song. Clearly, changing channels and finding a song in the midst of great turmoil will transform the condition.

ACTIVE IMAGINATION

Jung's concept of the active imagination is a strongly visual and auditory ritual. One hears and sees the image of a dream or fantasy figure.[1] In contrast to most meditation procedures which are more passively experienced, Jung recommended 'active' participation so that the student could interact and even conflict with his perceptions. This *'auseinandersetzung* with the unconscious', as Jung called it, changes both the observer and the material being worked with. Though active imagination usually takes the form of an internal dialogue, the student may also paint the dream experiences (see illustrations 3 and 4, which show the work of one of Jung's clients).

Process-oriented meditation extends active imagination so that it can be applied when the visual channel changes. If we are seeing a dream figure and we unconsciously start to move, it seems as if our image has disappeared. Our process has actually only changed channels. The information which appeared previously as a vision now appears in movement and processes itself in this channel. Jungians are extending active imagination into the realm of movement in a procedure called 'authentic movement' (Whitehouse 1979).

3 Jung's active imagination

a

b

c

4 A client's drawings
a Childhood disturbance
b Unlived life
c Confinement

Hidden Assumptions

KINAESTHESIS

Like proprioception, kinaesthesis, or movement, is rarely a developed channel for most of us. Movement and dance rituals are, however, extremely important to non-industrial communities (Wosien 1972). Everyone is aware of the altered state which occurs when you move to music. Ordinary life seems to stop as you sway to the sentiment or passion of a song.

Some well-known movement meditations such as walking meditation (focusing on the movements of the feet in vipasyana) seem to be a compensation for prolonged sitting meditations. T'ai chi is different: the dancer's motions are organized to enact a specific pattern, the cosmic Tao. The purpose of dervish spinning or whirling is to alter normal awareness, enabling the individual to experience the divine.

RELATIONSHIP

Relationship is also a channel of our perception since we often experience ourselves through others. Though body contact, seeing and talking obviously play an important part, relationship itself cannot be reduced to proprioception, visualization, movement or auditory phenomena because the human connection is more complex than the sum of its elementary parts.

Relationship, like kinaesthesis, proprioception and movement, is normally experienced as something which happens to us, not something we consciously do. The relationship meditations which I know of can be divided into two categories: body contact meditations and transference meditations involving a teacher or guru.

The idea that altered states and religious experiences occur while in sexual contact with another person is basic to Tantric yoga rituals where the partner experiences herself or himself as Shakti or Shiva (Rawson 1973). Apparently, the importance of sexual contact in these rituals has been overemphasized by western students. Nevertheless, the idea of Tantra is that love-making and yoga are combined, not to reach orgasm, but for each individual to experience totality. The yogi and his or her partner experience altered states by raising proprioception and heightening the sense of relationship.

Taoist yoga, also called Taoist alchemy, is a ritual in which partners stimulate one another sexually and attempt to integrate or extract yang or yin essence, the maleness or femaleness, from one another (Yu 1972). This practice has much in common with Tantra. Both rituals are somatic relationship experiences of what western psychology calls integration or contrasexual character-istics. Integration of any content or process alters consciousness by bringing new aspects of the personality to awareness. Tantra or Taoist alchemy brings the missing, opposite maleness or femaleness to the one-sided primary process.

Siddha yogis like Muktananda recommend a specific rela-tionship meditation in which the initiate worships the teacher (Muktananda 1974). This relationship meditation is also an integra-tion because it expands one's experience of life through assimilating qualities which have been transferred on to a teacher. Alteration in consciousness occurs through a switch of identities. Whereas before meditation one experienced oneself as an ordinary person, during meditation one sacrifices oneself to become a very powerful secondary figure, a god.

THE WORLD CHANNEL

For the American Indian, the world is a channel for information, just as dreams and body experiences are for other peoples. Mother Earth is, for the Indian, a channel and source of wisdom. The vision quest is the main North American Indian religious cere-mony; it is a quest for help and guidance from a higher power, the earth. The American Indian initiate may fast, sit quietly, meditate or discuss her problems with the tribal shaman, but her meditation inevitably includes a vision quest in which she goes out into nature to discover the wisdom missing in life. She listens to the trees, waits for a dream, watches for hallucinations or other unusual experiences, and then returns to the shaman and interprets the experience with him.[2]

MEDITATION: PROCESS AND TECHNIQUE

Some of the meditation procedures included in the foregoing have been:

1 Counting: closing the eyes and counting breaths
2 Walking: meditating upon the experiences of walking
3 The bubble: watching fantasies without taking part in them
4 Ascetic practice: restricting eating and sleeping
5 One-pointedness: focusing on one point such as a candle
6 Mantras: reciting a mantra or prayer
7 Yoga: doing hatha yoga and feeling your body
8 Prayer: assuming a philosophical stance such as 'be in the here and now', 'be a loving person', 'watch what you avoid', 'accept all as the Buddha'
9 Relationship: focusing on a loved one, teacher or guru
10 Vision quests: asking nature for help.

Channel blocking, channel switching, ignoring or undervaluing primary processes, and other means of creating altered states and 'stopping the world' occur naturally in everyone and need not be programmed into awareness. Learning how to follow their own process will enable people to discover these techniques within themselves, even if they have never read about or studied them before.

In the last chapter we defined meditation as picking up information appearing in specific channels. Many people meditate well with certain programmes because they are trained to stay in the specific channels of these programmes. They do not run into difficulties in meditation as long as their process remains in that channel. This tendency to develop awareness and familiarity in only certain channels and to ignore others is the basis of most meditation rituals. Staying in one channel gives you the sense of being on familiar ground and having reliable tools with which to work.

A disadvantage of staying in one channel, however, is that it leaves holes in awareness and creates unoccupied channels, places where meditation can go astray. This would not be the case if we understood that *meditation is a process which includes various techniques as they appear in the individual over time.*

Channel Changes and Disturbances

When we meditate with a specific channel or programme we experience disturbances as deviations from the path. We shall soon discover, however, that most disturbances are channel changes. My recommendation for people irritated by disturbances is that they increase their awareness of unused channels. For example, relationship meditation would be deepened by not only visualizing but also feeling, moving and sounding like the teacher. Hatha yoga students would be able to complete the yoga asanas more congruently if they were encouraged to follow some of their own body movements instead of sticking to a rigid programme.

Recognizing when processes switch to visualizations or relationship issues during massage would enrich the experience, even if the therapist merely asks about the vision or relationship issue. Dance therapy could benefit from bringing in body work with symptoms or dreams.

Yoga Teaches Yoga

In his *The Yoga Sutras*, Patanjali, one of the earliest Indian writers on yoga, says that meditation is its own teacher. 'Yoga teaches yoga,' he proclaimed (Patanjali 1953). I believe he meant that yoga, or any meditation technique, propagates itself after you have learned some of its fundamentals. Once you learn a given procedure, the meditation discipline itself generates greater awareness. In the beginning, however, it is helpful to learn from a teacher in order to be certain that we do not filter out important aspects of our awareness. But then, after a while, our own learning becomes the teacher of further learning.

If we follow our own inner process there will be times when we are required to visualize a mandala, drum on the floor, dance for God, count breaths, focus on an outer person, search the forest for answers, or love our partners. Our individual process may teach us every known ritual or plummet us into the depths of unknown experiences, as yet uncharted by the historians of meditation.

PART II
STEPS IN AWARENESS

Chapter 4

CHANNEL PERCEPTION

The following chapters were written in an altered state induced by meditating for long periods in the Swiss Alps and on the Oregon coast. Now, in a more ordinary state, I have decided to leave the work much as it occurred to me. I try simultaneously to explain and to do process-oriented meditation.

When I read this work now, I feel in conflict. Its lack of linearity and its frankness about my relationship with Barbara, my partner during those years, make me shy. Yet the following is the only way I could demonstrate the techniques of process-oriented meditation.

Here I sit, meditating in a Swiss mountain hut, 'Maiensass', 1,600 metres above sea level, 10 metres below the snowline. The hut, built in 1779, looks out upon a forest which covers the foot of an immense alp rising up into a glacier. The alp appears now and then as the mist around its peak parts for a moment, revealing its jagged white presence.

I hear cow-bells ringing. Cows on an alp, it is their vacation, their hour to ring, time to eat the summer's grass. I'm sitting in a Zen position on the ground in front of the old stall which faces my hut. This is my favourite writing position. It is drizzling very lightly, and I am wrapped in a rain outfit, a plastic tarp, and feel very, very heavy.

It is some time in mid-afternoon and I am writing as part of a meditation. The fog drifts across the grey, uneven roof of the hut. I think about *Working with the Dreaming Body*, a book I have just completed for the general public. I want to be as simple and straightforward here as I was there.

Psychotherapy, as I see it, is a procedure in which you use a trained therapist to help you with your life by depending, more or less, upon his or her awareness of psychophysical processes which you may not be aware of in yourself. In therapy, you let go and someone else sees, hears, and helps you feel yourself. In process-oriented meditation, you learn how to become a trained observer capable of helping yourself with your own feelings, visions, voices, relationships, movements, and body problems.

The basic idea of inner dreambody work is that whatever you are able to experience contains its own evolution, solution and growth. The stuff of your visions, voices and body pains is not maya, not an illusion, but an express train to yourself.

Now I am indoors, eating a banana, slowly. I can no longer afford to eat without being aware. How many bananas have gone through me, leaving effects which I have not noticed? My stomach . . . I hear the fire in the ceramic oven crackling away. I see in my mind's eye the old seminar house in Les Diableret and remember how my meditation studies began, or how my meditation begins now.

SUFFERING AND AWARENESS

The great world religions, Buddhism and Christianity, suggest that awareness begins in pain. Christianity says we suffer because we follow our drives. Buddhism says that life is suffering and pain. Although many people begin psychotherapy today without a particular reason, there is no way of getting round the issue of pain. Growth and insight begin most often with dissatisfaction, unhappiness and pain. You would think, as I have often, that pain would be sufficient motivation for change. I used to assume that people would change if they had to. Then, after many years of therapeutic work, I made a disturbing discovery that shook my belief in people.

I discovered that pain was not enough to motivate people to change; its presence or absence alone is not sufficient to change people. There is something else, a strange, unpredictable element which is required before people can work out problems and alter their lives. This element is a mixture of discipline, love and enlightenment.

THE WARRIOR'S ELEMENT

A warrior-like discipline is helpful in working alone on oneself and getting through a difficult spot. Discipline is a subtle thing which you cannot develop by simply being interested. Discipline is an inner drive which pushes you.

The warrior's discipline is connected to wonder and love. It begins with wonder and curiosity. If something attracts you, if you love it, you'll find the necessary discipline to study it and discover its nature. If human nature does not attract you, you will always find reasons for avoiding the discovery of yourself and others.

For some, discipline is reminiscent of harsh parental control. For these people, self-discipline is a chore they would rather avoid; they complain that fatigue or lack of time prevents them from disciplining themselves. Yet enforced discipline and working against fatigue are not the kind of discipline I am talking about.

If your process fascinates you, you will become aware of the continuum of awareness, of the process which organizes existence. The process itself will fascinate you with its power, and this excitement creates discipline.

Many of us learn discipline because we are in love with this universe. We have such wondrous beginners' minds that we can meditate without identifying it as such. We focus on people and objects around us. Belief and wonder guide us in a quiet way to do things normally associated with highly disciplined people. If you ask them how they made such insightful and powerful decisions, they either do not know or may answer, as one person did, 'My heart just knew.'

Discipline, wonder, love and enlightenment are all parts of the warrior's art in meditation.

A DREAM

For a moment I am well. I feel relaxed, happy. I hear a stream nearby, the cars on a distant road. I see a dream I had last night in which someone wanted to reach a goal but discovered that he had already reached it. Writing today is an experiment. I do not know what wants to speak. I wait and meditate, and what you are reading is the result.

I sit on my heels and write on a pad placed on a tree stump about $2\frac{1}{2}$ feet high. To my right – to my surprise – I see a woman and two small children approaching my isolated hut. I hear the kids making funny noises. I feel how I brace myself inwardly to face them by tightening my neck and shoulders. 'You always want the world your way, no visitors,' says an inner voice. Was this the voice, the information locked up in my tight muscles? I realized that my writing was a goal I had set and was trying to fulfil, and that everything else was a disturbance. An old problem. My muscles relax.

Now I find myself looking to the right again. What? The triad should be near my house, but no, they have disappeared. I find myself getting up and leaving my writing. My body is doing this all by itself. Why? What has this to do with my dream? This question gives me an 'aha!'. My goal today has been reached. The person in my dream who had a goal and had already reached it was me. As soon as I am able to pick up what is happening, I am at the goal, the end. Do you know what I mean? See you tomorrow.

THE FIRST STEP

Today I went running in the alps and got lost. I went too far, running up one side of a mountain, over the top, and then following the wind, around the back, down the side, discovering an alpine lake. Trying to return, I got lost. How should I get back? As I strained against the altitude and mountain grade, I went just a bit over my physical edge, my kinaesthetic limits. At that moment a picture came to me. I saw myself alone and unable to go on. Suddenly, in my vision, I found what Don Juan calls 'personal power', a physical force which takes me beyond my normal energy.[1] I began to run again and unexpectedly found my way back.

I experience meditation as a multi-channelled process which is at work all the time, once you master its basic steps. I am going to describe the first step in the method, namely, discovering the channel.

Stop whatever you are doing and close your eyes. Sit still for a moment and ask yourself one, and only one, question.

What channel am I in?

Are you *feeling* something proprioceptively in your body? Are you *seeing* something with your inner or outer eyes? Are you *hearing* anything?

The channel question is the basis of meditation. If you know the channel you are perceiving in, you need not programme your meditation, but can find out the programme which wants to happen today. You are already at your goal. If you know *how* you perceive something, then you can work with your process; you can follow the unfolding of your body, mind, relationships and dreams. If you do not know how you are perceiving, your perceptions function autonomously, just like dreams.

Thus, asking about channels makes you aware of your awareness. Any time you ask yourself which channel you are in, you begin to meditate. If you get lost in your work, simply ask, 'What channel am I in now?'

Right now my focus of awareness is (visually) absorbed by seeing Barbara come and sit next to me. How nice to see her. I notice (proprioceptively) my body shyly tighten ... it wants to write. I hear (auditory) a voice tell my body, 'Take her in and imagine that she is the reader. Talk to your reader. Do not keep her out of the work.' I find my body relaxing. What a pleasure!

You will notice that I use many different channels. I talk of running, of walking, eating, looking outside, of feeling my body, hearing voices and of relationship. All of these channels are different aspects of the same message expressing itself in many different ways. They are all parts of one process in conflict and harmony with itself.

The reason I recommended that you begin your meditation with only three channels, seeing, hearing and feeling, is because these are the most frequently used and familiar introverted channels. But wait . . . I cannot go on with my discussion right now. Hold on a moment. I just heard a piece of wood fall to my right. A piece came off a nicely stacked-up pile. I listened, got scared, felt my body and imagined a wood spirit had arrived. It said, 'Yes, I am here, I am a peasant at work. I am my work. It is simple, straightforward. Believe in it.'

I wish I believed more in my work. I am recommending something simple, too: that my reader trust and follow the inner process. You need not trust any human being, not even me. I have as yet to meet a guru or wise, enlightened, educated, shamanic, mediumistic person who is as intelligent as the process which unfolds in the channels of your own perception.

ALCHEMY

Thank God Jung dug up the alchemists. They would have loved process-oriented meditation. In fact it is exactly what they did. They worked with the unknown, calling it *scientia*, meaning science, knowledge, or information. They worked with their *scientia* by meditating on what they did not know. This unknown they called the *prima materia*, the basic substance which turned into gold when cooked. They opened up to the unknown but did not have very good vessels to work with. They thought the *prima materia* was chemical matter, not process or information occurring in their own channels of perception. What will the future think about our limited vessels of today?

KEEP STILL AND CLOSE YOUR EYES

To begin with, try closing your eyes and keeping still when you ask yourself which channel you are in. Block out extraverted seeing and kinaesthesis. Use three channels: inner seeing, hearing and body feeling. Do this for a few minutes at your leisure.

I recommend that you do not use your outer visual channel, because looking is like movement. It happens too spontaneously. Your eyes and limbs move without awareness, without focusing. They flit from one thing to another with the speed of light without you even realizing that you are looking at something. Your eyes are doing 'rapid eye movements', day and night, dreaming all the time. You are fascinated by things which you need to become; you gaze at objects and people you dislike because you need more contact with them in yourself.

Your body moves continually and unconsciously in order to avoid discomfort. If you close your eyes and stop kinaesthesia, you become aware of your thinking, hearing and seeing. You will be pressed to examine the source of your discomforts and pleasures, the essence of your proprioception. Your movement reacts to pain so quickly that if you do not inhibit your motion, you may never get the chance to realize what your biological life is in conflict with. You will also miss the opportunity to integrate the healing function in yourself, that is, your body's tendency to move away from pain.

When you open your eyes after fifteen minutes, your movements and vision will be slowed down, and you will be able to investigate them more exactly. Later on I will work on these and other channels with you, but first I want to speak more about working with visualizing, hearing and body feeling.

Chapter 5

AMPLIFICATION

Think of an alchemist taking the *prima materia*, his process, and cooking it. In process terms, turning up the fire under the pot is amplifying a signal in the channel in which it occurs. Once you become aware of which channel you are perceiving in, the next step is to amplify your perception. Amplifying a process contains it and allows it to unfold at its own tempo. The basic idea is to help the process unravel, to develop as fully as possible, so that it will reveal its own hidden message.

WORKING WITH VISUALIZATION

Thus, if you are seeing, see even more. See your inner visions more clearly, more exactly, notice the colours, watch for certain figures, examine their peculiarities, see all the movements. Approach your visions as if they needed encouragement. Dream your visions to conclusion. Coach yourself while visualizing. Say, 'Yes, dream on, wonderful, and what happens now, and look at that, etc.'

You began working with closed eyes. As your eyes open, notice carefully what happens. How do they open? Are you seeing humans, plant life, mountains, are you in a room? Look around the room. Notice what you look at. Now you are using your extraverted seeing. Most people are blind in that they do not notice what they see. Ask yourself why your vision fastens on to a particular person or object.

Notice what happens when you cannot see something. Instead of changing the object of your focus, moving closer to or away

47

from the object, stay with being nearsighted or farsighted. What does the blurring do to you, for you? If you stay with this phenomenon long enough, you may notice that your inability to focus may be related to your need to fantasize more, to fill in missing information with inner intuitions and images. Perhaps you are really a medium and have never developed your intuitive abilities before. Now your eyes are helping you. Who is looking? Who uses your eyes? Who is behind them? Is it you or an eagle?

AMPLIFYING HEARING

Notice when you hear things. Are you hearing outer or inner sounds? Do you hear an internal dialogue? Listen carefully. Who is talking? Is it a male or female voice, old or young, harsh or sweet, menacing or apologetic? Amplify these sounds in your own individual way. Listen to what happens.

Consider the possibility that you only hear that which you do not know or do not accept in yourself. Can you hear things which are not right for you, or forget that which you do not need to know? If you have hearing or memory problems, you have them for a good reason. Try having them consciously and enjoy them.

When you do hear and see, you are hearing and seeing exactly the right thing, that which will bring you some new information. If you already had this knowledge or information, you might not be hearing it again.

Take the material which stays long enough to catch and amplify it; make it louder, clearer, more beautiful or horrible, melodious, staccato, rhythmic or non-rhythmic. From which ear do you seem to be hearing? Or do you hear through your back like some people? I will bet there are intricacies to your hearing which you have never dreamed about.

Later, when you are more advanced in meditation, you will notice that your inner sounds change channels and you may start to move, dance or sing. That is wonderful. I will speak more fully of channel changes later.

INTERNAL CRITICISM

Internal dialogue often resembles a non-stop talker. Non-stop talking frequently happens because the talker is not being heard. Some aspect of the internal dialogue, perhaps a particular plea or a problem, is not being heard. Many people hate working on themselves alone and avoid it because they cannot stand their internal voices. They know that if they go internal, they are going to meet with some form of self-hatred or self-criticism. When you discover a nasty voice, listen to it exactly before changing channels. Later on I will tell you different ways of dealing with these voices.

BODY FEELING

When it comes to proprioception, each body is different. Your tolerance of pain, for instance, is dependent upon how much you feel. Some people who are aware of feeling very little are unusually afraid of or very sensitive to physical pain.

Your beginning awareness of proprioception usually consists of indiscriminate and vague information, such as feeling well or sick, heavy or sad. The first step in working with proprioception is to feel your body on its own terms. It is full of sensitivity which only you can feel. Feel all the sensations. It might be helpful for you to start from the bottom. Feel your feet, your lower and upper legs. Feel anything which comes to your attention. Feel your pelvic region, your buttocks, your genital region. Do you notice hot or cold spots, tension and pressure? What about your lower back and your stomach? Move your stomach around a bit and notice what it feels like. Do you notice your heart beat in your chest, or any tension in your shoulders? Does your skin itch? What parts are warm or cool? How does your head feel?

Steps in Awareness

Your body is built in a certain way; it can have diseases and experiences which others can never know about. It can also experience archetypal postures, feelings and movements which are common to everyone. Nevertheless, though it has much in common with other bodies, yours may have more individual peculiarities than you know.

As you develop your body sensitivity in meditation you will begin to react to things which you don't usually notice, like slight variations in room temperature or pressures from clothing or altitude. You become sensitive to experiences which you had previously never felt. You will get closer to the dreaming process and notice exactly how you create depressions and unhappiness in your physical body.

Once you notice you are propriocepting temperature, hot and cold, pain, a full stomach or headache, you can cook your feelings. The most powerful way to propriocept is to keep still because movement relieves sensations before they get a chance to reach your awareness. Be still and feel.

Symptoms

If you have a symptom, what luck, for you can amplify it. Feel it in great detail, notice how the pain radiates out into your body. In which direction does it go? Feel the associated temperatures, the hot and the cold, the shivering, the pressures, light-headedness, the nausea. Examine where the nausea originates. Amplify the intensity of your focus until you could, if you had to, tell someone else the details of your body experience. Tell them in such a way that they could reproduce the symptoms themselves. If you cannot recreate such detail, then your proprioception may be incomplete.

Inner Doctors

If you meditate well in the proprioceptive channel, you can work on many, perhaps even all, of your symptoms by yourself. You might be able to find your own inner doctor. A woman in a recent

50

meditation seminar came down with a fever and cold during her meditation. She amplified her proprioception and felt as if someone were knifing her in the throat. She worked with the experience of being knifed and consequently felt better. That night she dreamed that she met an inner doctor with magical medicine.

I recently went on a vision quest. I went to a special spot at the base of a glacier and meditated to find the information in my seeing, hearing, feeling and moving. I saw a vision of a glacier man, beyond time, talking to me. I listened to him closely and he told me that the meaning of all human life, not just my personal life, was to become a channel for the cosmic process. Just as our eyes and ears are channels for us to become aware of, so we are the eyes and ears for the universe. He said that the meaning of human life was to become a perfect channel for the evolution of our universe. Rocks, trees and animals, as well as mountains and rivers, are other special channels. Are we the only channels who can consciously amplify and follow our changes? Becoming aware and amplifying awareness may well be our full-time job.

He told me, and I am still proving this to myself, that the purpose of having a human body is to channel the universal spirit in a very special way. Everybody has his own individual nature because of his individual task in this life as a channel. The greatest pain in life is not knowing your task as a channel and not allowing or appreciating your specific body to fulfil its own purpose and nature.

Were his statements only valid for me in that moment or are they universally true? Each should form his or her own visions and beliefs.

BODY TYPES

An overweight man who cannot lose an ounce worked in one of my meditation seminars. He let himself move slowly to amplify his movements. His body did the candle asana (he lay on his back, raised his legs, and braced his hips with his hands, his elbows flat against the floor, until his legs pointed vertically upwards). Then he went into the plough asana (see illustrations 5a and 5b, which show the famous hatha yoga teacher B. K. S. Iyengar demonstrating the postures). His stomach was in the way when his legs tried to go over to the floor, yet his body wanted this position! The weight made it impossible for him to breathe. He amplified the proprioceptive experience by staying in the plough until he could not bear it any longer. Then he had a vision. Channels change automatically if you amplify sensations as much as possible, in this case from proprioception to visualization. In his vision he saw the Michelin advertisement with the powerful man standing beneath a tyre. He said the tyre was soft on the outside but had an iron core within.

He apparently needs his weight to help him realize that he himself is a long-lasting, powerful Michelin tyre, soft on the outside but strong within. He was surprised by this vision because he had suspected that he was weak. I imagine this man to be capable of channelling a particular part of this universe, that aspect of this world which speaks softly but has an iron core of wisdom within it.

This man's body is just what he needs. Diet or exercise pro-grammes are not enough. He needs an awareness of his inner strength.

In another meditation seminar, a very tall man followed his inclination to move during a meditation. He soon found himself becoming a giant. As he rose from a sitting position, he had a vision of standing high above the world, rising above his mother, he said, who wanted to hold him down and stop him from loving. This man needs his great height in order to transcend his mother and other forces within and outside of him which do not want him to love. As he moved, he spontaneously and naturally moved into the yoga position called the 'mountain' (see illustration 6). Each body is special, as these examples show, and having your body fully, being what you feel in your body is your job in this world.

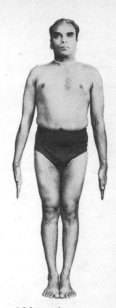

5a Candle asana

6 Mountain asana

5b Plough asana

MOVEMENT

After you have meditated for a half hour without moving or opening your eyes, I recommend that you investigate your movement channel, kinaesthesis. Movement can be connected to the other channels or experienced all by itself. Some dancers, the most gifted movers, frequently do not feel, see or hear, but simply follow their movement sense.

To find out about movement, begin first by meditating on your feeling, seeing and hearing as you have been doing, and amplifying these experiences. Then studiously follow your minute tendencies to move. Start with slow movements. If you are sitting in a lotus position, you might find yourself moving back and forth (see illustration 7). Notice your desire to bend forwards and backwards, to relieve your back muscles. Notice what happens in your neck, your jaws, inside your mouth. Notice what sort of movements happen in your throat as you sway from side to side. If you find yourself getting up, then get up in such a way that it becomes the most fascinating thing you have ever done. Examine and investigate your movement. Notice how your joints creak, discover where they are! Investigate your movement machinery, your tendons, inner muscles, even the inner abdominal experiences which help you move. If you move slowly enough, you will have a full-time job just moving a centimetre in any direction. This kind of movement is an absolute altered state. Enjoy it. If you stand up, notice what happens. Stand up completely. Stand first on one leg, then on the other. Which carries more weight when you stand on both? Do you bounce slowly from one to the other? Do you start to walk? If you begin to walk, find out about your feet, notice the muscles and bones in them.

YOGA AND MOVEMENT

This kind of slow movement meditation develops yoga; it is the beginning of hatha yoga. The positions you move from, the ones you move into and stay in, are almost always classical asanas. It

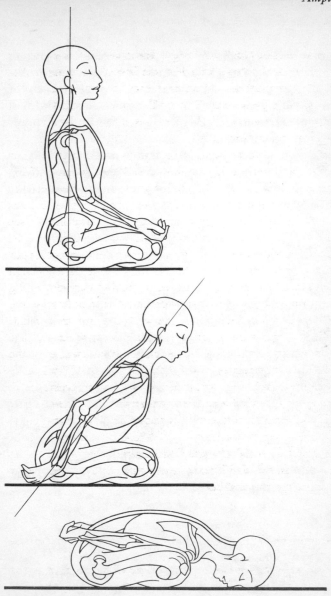

7 Sitting and moving

seems very likely to both Barbara and me that slow movement meditation is the way hatha yoga developed. Yogis began to move and found that their bodies needed, for whatever reasons, to assume certain positions. The names of the yoga asanas, cat, cobra, bow, etc., indicate how these positions correspond to specific images and feelings.

Amplifying movement and body feeling, kinaesthesis and proprioception, produces a sort of original or archaic yoga, a process-oriented yoga. We could also call it introverted body work or process work. It is letting your body dream. Amplify movements, follow them, bring them as far as they want to go and notice what happens (see illustrations 8–13).

CHANNEL CHANGES

At the limits of your movements, the physical edges of your body, are secondary processes, your dreams and your dreambody. Try taking your movements to their limits and investigate your edges (to be discussed in greater detail in the next chapter), the limitations of your individual body. Be very gentle with the way you approach your physical limits, as it is possible to pull a muscle without realizing it until later. The purpose of this work is not to accomplish a physical feat but to discover who you are. Meditate, but do not push at the edge. Approach your physical limits carefully and then hold that position.

At this point changing the channels of your experience will give you greater information about the process you are involved with kinaesthetically. Try the following experiment. Ask yourself to see the experience you are now feeling. The resulting vision is your biological dream, your power stance of the moment.

Movement is full of process and information. Do not abuse movement by programming it or even by letting it just happen. Pick up the movements which happen to you spontaneously, amplify them, take them to their limits and then change channels to increase your awareness of what your body is doing.

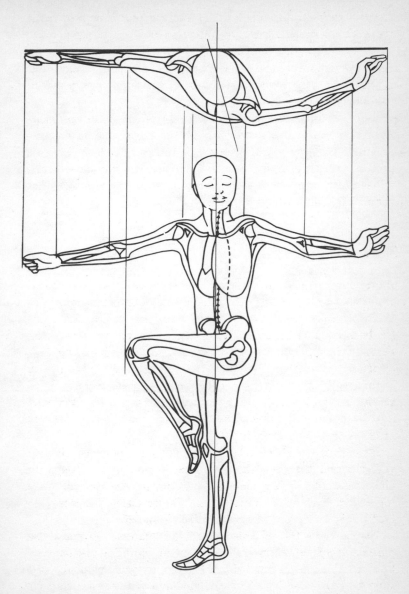

8 Twisting

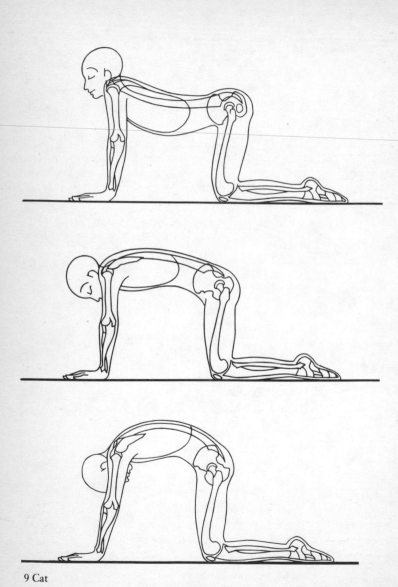

9 Cat

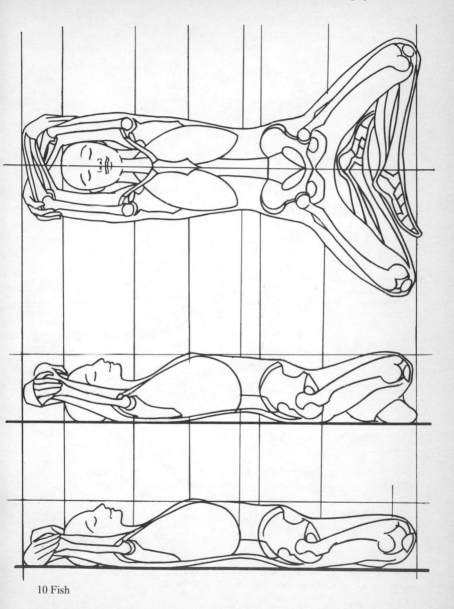

10 Fish

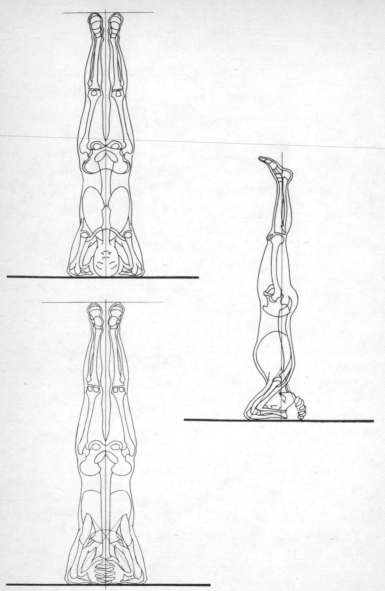

11 Headstand

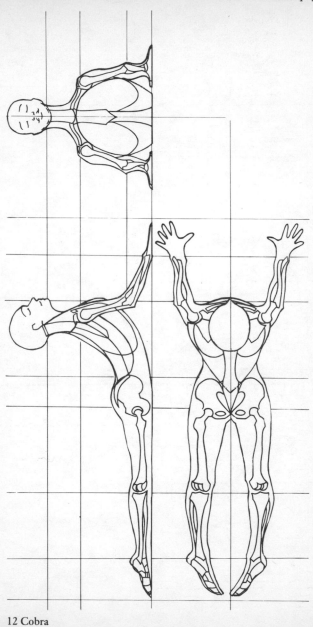

12 Cobra

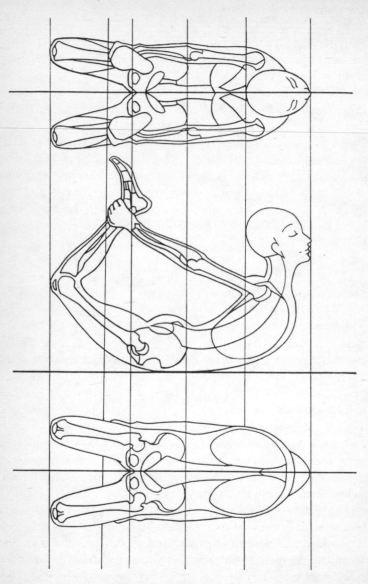

13 Bow

MY BODY

I am not very flexible physically. Recently, while doing yoga with Barbara, I discovered that I hated the bow, that is, reaching backwards and grabbing my ankles while rolling on my tummy on the floor (see illustration 13). How I detest this position! I held on to my ankles for as long as I could, straining against myself and then, bang, I switched channels and saw a picture, a vision. And what was it? Iron Hans, the fairy-tale character! I saw the neglected shadow of western civilization, the wild man, the rough forest personality cast out by modern civilization, archetypal primitive man. At my edge of physical movement was the vision of the rough guy, the iron man who will not yield, who is intent upon being himself. This is the information that was stored in my tight tendons, the meaning of my inflexibility.

SECONDARY AND MYOCLONIC MOVEMENT

There are many movements that happen so quickly that we have trouble perceiving them. They are myoclonic, that is, they are like the twitches and jerky movements you have when you are falling asleep. You may be dreaming you are falling down the stairs, your body twitches as it falls, and then bang! you are awake.

Likewise, when you are meditating or nearing the hypnagogic level of experience where visions and voices occur, your body is under the direction of your dreaming power and it moves in the same spontaneous way as when you dream and hear voices. So be quick! Pick up these incomplete movements, amplify them, and follow them to completion whenever possible.

The more aware you are of your movements, the more you will be able to differentiate between primary process movement, which is intended and which completes itself in a meaningful way, and secondary movement, which has a myoclonic character. If you can catch your secondary process in the movement channel, you can almost always connect to the dreams you had the night before.

Movement differentiation is important because if you try to perform 'authentic movement' or, being creative and spontaneous, dance with the hope of doing this in an original way, you will probably not be able to do so. The secondary, incomplete and incomprehensible movements are the direct road to authentic, creative and unpredictable dream dancing. It is in these movements, outside of our intent, that the information of our dreams is found.

I recently worked with a man on the process of walking. His primary movement was walking. Yet, as he walked, he became aware that he walked like a robot. He said it was necessary to walk like that in order to keep himself under control. His primary process, the one he identified with, was control; his secondary process was to be out of control. I recommended that he practise his control, thinking that it must be there for a good reason. As we worked on his walking, he suddenly told me that he suffered from *grand mal* epilepsy.

Now, which comes first, the chicken or the egg? Was his control a protection against *grand mal* seizures, or were the seizures a compensatory response to the control? In process work, we entertain causal questions, but prefer to make hypotheses based on the process at hand. So I asked him if he would like us to experience together the out-of-control process which was in his epilepsy. He agreed, and creative movement came out, and then, suddenly, anger, too. He was angry about early childhood experiences. We amplified the angry movements, and a dance, a beautiful and graceful martial arts dance, ensued. Locked up in his epileptic, secondary movements were defence, rage, offence and power.

When this man walks, several processes walk with him. There is the one who walks controlling emotions, and there is another who is angry and out of control. And in process work, there is the one who processes both of these figures, combining them in a fluid dance of life marrying control with abandon. Two states frozen in time, control and abandon, became, as Don Juan would say, the warrior's art, 'controlled abandon'. Process-oriented movement meditation gives us rapid access to unknown states and creative integration as well.

MOVEMENT FOR ITS OWN SAKE

There will be times in meditation when you will find yourself moving in such a way that nothing happens other than the movement. No channel changes. You may roll back and forth, or constantly bend over backwards. The interesting thing about these movements and positions is that they are not accompanied by statements from other channels. These are movements of and for themselves. Their only purpose seems to be a healing function. When done with consciousness, you can notice how this healing function works by massaging tight and fearful places in your body.

Working in the movement channel is one of the singularities of process-oriented meditation. Continuous willingness to move differentiates this work from certain eastern rituals which integrate the need for movement, for example by recommending that the initiate get up periodically to complete a programmed walking movement.

PROCESS IMMERSION

Once you feel at home with your process, walking breaks won't be necessary in meditation because movement awareness makes it possible to remain in a place the size of a yoga mat for hours at a time without the need to get up and stretch. During these hours, you may allow your process to switch channels, first listening to voices, then seeing dream figures, having insights, writing them down on paper, going back to sitting, then swaying, standing, shaking, lying down and even sleeping. When this is done over the course of several days, you get more and more deeply involved in your process until it becomes a part of life itself. This process immersion itself appears to be the goal which the body wanted in the first place, but which we were unaware of. Whatever happens during the ritualized time of meditation, be it five minutes or five hours, is a glimpse of how life might be lived – wondrously!

A butterfly has just now landed on my pen. I continue to write, slowly, with it on my pen. Its rhythmic movements make it difficult for me to see my handwriting. Am I a butterfly? As I meditate on the butterfly, I see that it is lighter than me. A fair observer is now writing to you and realizes that the 'I' of the previous sentence who is writing and meditating is my primary process while the butterfly who is blocking my writing is my secondary one. Time to stop writing and find out more about the butterfly!

Chapter 6
EDGES

Disturbances, restlessness and wandering focus have been the central meditation problems throughout the ages. The endless turning of the karmic wheel, the movement of the mind, the coming and going of voices, movements, visions, aches, pain, material possessions and relationships have been considered the meditator's greatest foe. Process work evaluates these changes and interruptions differently. The indomitable disturbances are due to two factors which will be discussed in this chapter: channel changes and edges.

THE INVARIANT MESSAGE

An edge is reached when a process brings up information which is difficult for you to accept. Channels switch when an edge has been reached or when it is time to develop awareness in different areas. The information remains the same; the message is constant, but the channels change. In both cases, the surprising thing is that the mind does not really wander at all. You can try to fix your attention on one process if you feel that you must, as is the ideal of many meditations, but you actually don't need to because the same message repeats itself in a different channel each time your focus changes.

THE CONSERVATION OF PROCESS

Something I learned years ago from dream work was that though the scenes in a dream change, each scene carries essentially the same message. 'Process is neither created nor destroyed, but is always conserved' is how a scientist would express this fact. Process disappears from conscious focus only to reappear in a channel unoccupied by conscious awareness. The message changes a bit as soon as you pick it up. Your dreams may tell you to take a risk, your movements may lead you to trip and almost fall, your body may threaten you with serious symptoms, and your relationships may provoke you to take risks. Once you take a risk, however, the message, which had been appearing in all possible channels, changes.

What then creates the changes in our visions, body experience and movements? It could be the drive to become whole, to know yourself and develop awareness in all channels.

The mysterious point which I call the edge is a road-block in a given channel. At that point your process changes channels and leaves your awareness hanging. For example, you dream about someone you do not like, a woman you cannot bear to look at because she incorporates all the negative qualities you hate the most. You have an edge against her. Thus, when you work on your dream, you tend to look for other parts of the dream which are more appealing. Later you run into the same kind of negative person in a neighbourhood store. Now the figure is located in the world channel, but the message is the same: *Look at and experience your negative qualities*.

At the edge in the visual channel there appears to be a deviation from seeing. You would normally think that you are distracted, but if you meditate further you notice that another channel – the world – begins to work, carrying the same message. The same process begins anew in another channel.

CYCLING

It may even happen that the same visual process repeats itself. You once again get to the same edge of hating negative qualities and you cycle and cycle, as if on a karmic wheel. You keep repeating, persevering, revolving around some mysterious point without realizing that behind your cycling is an edge to the message. If you want to get off the wheel, then you have to meet the edge and go over it. But this is no simple business, because when you get to the edge, processes switch, channels change, your meditation flickers, and awareness gets cloudy. Now you are working alone in the darkness of meditation. Catch your edges, hold them and get to know them.

CATCHING THE EDGE

There are various ways of finding out more about these mysterious and invisible edges which organize your meditations. I know several ways of doing this. One way is to amplify processes in the channels in which they occur and catch the moment they change channels or content. Then go back to investigate when and where they changed.

This moment of change is a remarkable one; it is here that you meet the karmic wheel, the great mystery of confusion and mercuriality. To catch this moment you must be quick. Switching happens so rapidly and with such unconsciousness that you will need to be an expert to catch the edge which structured the change. Edges are very, very slippery. I think the most straightforward way to catch these tricky edges is simply to wonder about them. A useful method of investigating the edge phenomenon is to meditate upon the following questions. Write down the answers to these questions, meditate on those too, and you will understand the structure of many autonomous processes in yourself.

1 What vision, figure, object or scene can you almost not bear to look at?
2 What do you not like hearing? Which tones or voices do you detest?
3 What feelings, emotions, physical sensations or body parts can you almost not bear to focus upon?

4 What movements seem to be forbidden to you?
5 What relationship issues would you like to avoid, and which people do you hate?
6 What world situation do you avoid or is beyond your ability to comprehend and tolerate?

DREAMING AT THE EDGE

If you write down the answers to these questions, then you will be able to find out or even guess what you are going to dream, for dreams circulate around edges, around the interaction between primary and secondary processes. If you know your edges in the various channels, you can guess the accidental and creative movements, the synchronicities, the relationship troubles and the kinds of psychosomatic body experiences you will have. By writing down these edges, meditating on them and staying close to them, you are working on core problems which organize your process, your personal myth.

Knowing your edges can also enable you to make the following divinatory experiment. Once you have written down the edges, write down your primary process – that is, the behaviour which is disturbed by these edges. If you do not like a given person, what part of you does not like this person? What part of your own behaviour cannot tolerate this person? This is your primary process.

The next step is to throw the *I Ching*, but before you do so, try to guess the hexagram you will get by using your answers to the above questions. One reader wrote the following:

I did the exercise and guessed the hexagram. I thought it would be something with aggression, and I got Hexagram 6, 'Conflict', in the *I Ching*. As visual edges I had written: 'downhill ski racing, boxing, war and killing'. The following night I dreamed of people shooting at the house I was in with a machine gun, and of two men skiing straight down a steep slope.

It is interesting to note that her visual edges also imply a kin-aesthetic edge (skiing), a world edge (war), and a relationship edge (boxing). This exercise shows that the edges in the various channels are related and structure synchronistic events such as the *I Ching* and dreams. If you know your edges, you can predict a lot about your life!

DEFINITION OF EDGES

Now that you have had some experiential contact with edges, I want to define them again because of their importance. *Edges are names for the experience of confinement, for the limitations in awareness, for the boundaries of your own identity*. The most common edges are found at the limits of the primary process. A statement of identity, such as 'I am not that', indicates an edge. Thus, going over an edge is always an immense experience; you feel that your identity is changing, confused, lost or challenged.

Secondary processes can also be delimiting. If you have been a sweet person, your secondary process, which you used to have an edge against, is to be tougher and less sensitive. You find yourself not wanting to be sweet any more, in fact you have an edge against it! Both primary and secondary processes have edges which keep them separated from one another. If you work on your edges, you become, momentarily at least, a fluid person.

LIBERATION

The terms 'enlightenment' and 'freedom' imply flexibility and openness. 'Liberation' in process language means being aware of your edges and being able to move with them or around them. Liberation implies becoming free of your edges to your secondary process (which means being tough if you want to), and to your primary process (which means being sweet when necessary). Liberation is detachment from edges, from the cycling processes which give you the repetitive, hopeless and bored experience of life.

Process concepts understand liberation within the paradigm of change, not as a goal to be obtained and held on to, but as another momentary state in an ever-changing kaleidoscope. There are many ways to reach this state. You can analyse your dreams and recognize the secondary processes you need. You can do hatha yoga and work on your movement edges there and go over them. I gave an example in the last chapter of Iron Hans, a figure who appeared at one of my kinaesthetic edges. Working on him allowed me to move in new ways over the edge. You can do relationship work, discover the edges blocking you from another person, go over this edge and have a new experience of freedom in love and friendship. You can work with the world, find your confining edges and begin to free yourself on this planet.

WORKING AT THE EDGE

Simple hope and encouragement may be enough to get you over an edge. One way to help yourself over edges in meditation is by imagining a dream figure who could get over the edge you cannot. Or you can recall how you got over such edges in the past. Simple encouragement may be enough to get you over an edge. Or you can stay at the edge and wait to see how your process deals with it. The desire for freedom from an edge is always accompanied by some internal pattern (such as encouragement, a dream figure or a memory) for crossing the borders into unknown territory.

When at an edge, instead of being thrown around by the confusion of channel and content changes, you yourself can deliberately move back and forth, change channels or use your occupied and unoccupied channels. If your mind is wandering, consciously switch channels. If you get stuck in one channel, hearing for instance, change channels and make a picture or dance what you have heard.

EDGES AND SYMPTOMS

If you hold on to the phenomena which occur at the edge, you can get a sensory experience of how physical diseases, relationship problems, chronic life problems and the myth of your personal existence are created. You meet the part of yourself which is hypnotized: the edge is generated by a belief which does not correspond to objective reality. Let me give an example. A man who had chronic bladder and prostate trouble decided to work on his symptoms in a meditation. He gave me the following report:

> I sat in meditation for a long time. After a while, I began to feel my bladder, the problem the doctors referred to as a prostate problem. This time I decided to discover why I could not stay with the problem and work on any edges. I noticed that I was constantly disturbed by noises. My wife broke into the meditation room with my daughter, both joked about my sitting so seriously. They left. I meditated upon my family as a disturbance, as a secondary process not going along with my primary one, as you always recommend. I thought they must be a secondary process, but I could not understand yet what that could be. Were they meant to disturb my seriousness? How could they be 'the way'?
>
> I continued. I decided not to get up and urinate but to let my body experience take me to an edge. I sat and sat, and the proprioceptive experience of bladder pressure began to get greater and greater. I felt that I would explode. I grew fearful that I would burst and die. I decided to go on. Suddenly I was filled with an immense red feeling, and became a balloon bursting out – out of all of my inhibitions, from the world itself.
>
> Freedom, the feeling of immense freedom and happiness overcame me! I took great deep breaths. I got up and danced, crying with happiness and spinning around like a mad man. I knew then that my fears of dying which had plagued me all of my life, all of my attempts and cramping to

create a secure position for myself on this earth, were useless. I knew that my freedom was freedom from these security drives. I ran out to the kitchen where my family was sitting, and in a great rush told them that we would all go on vacation. At first they thought I had gone mad but then they all agreed with pleasure!

With difficulty I decided to admit that I needed their joking, that they were right about how serious I was, not only with meditation, but with many other things as well. To my surprise, instead of laughing at me as they always did in the past, my wife cried and we all cried together. The planned prostate operation was put off for the time being, since the cramping in that area disappeared.

This man's report indicates that his first edge was to investigate the pain and pressure in his bladder. He probably thought he would explode or die if he went into these feelings. The second edge he went over was the belief that he was responsible for making life go on. He thought that if he did not promote his security he would die. What he called a bladder or prostate cramp was experienced in meditation as a pressure trying to break free of the drive for security.

CHANNEL CHANGES AND DEVELOPMENT

Processes switch and confuse you, not only because they run into edges, but because they are organized by the drive to develop awareness in channels which have not been previously used.

For example, in a meditation, a woman started to doze off and suddenly had a vision of a lightning bolt. This bolt gave her a shock, and she felt herself awakening. As she focused on and amplified the vision of the lightning bolt, a voice suddenly said, 'Kill the past . . . like a bolt of lightning.' But she was still too tired to follow this recommendation; it was an edge. So she continued to listen to it, repeating it to herself, amplifying its tone. Her fatigue came back again, and this time she found herself focusing upon her body. She felt it and found herself moving into a particular yoga asana called the fish (see illustration 10, page 59). She did the fish, amplified it by opening up her pelvis even more, and she suddenly became aware of a rash in her groin. Ouch . . . aha! She made a discovery. The lightning now took place in her groin as a fiery rash. Thus, the same message appeared in the vision, the voice and the rash; she came to the edge of one channel, and the message reappeared in another channel. At this point, she jumped up and was ready to consider the changes she needed to make in her life.

Her meditation began with fatigue, that is, a proprioceptive experience. She amplified this process and switched it into a vision, and at the edge of the vision of the lightning bolt a channel change occurred and she heard a voice telling her to change. What was represented in this voice then appeared in her proprioception of the rash, and finally in her movement, jumping up and being ready to make the changes.

From a causal viewpoint, we can say that the channel switching occurred because she felt unable to change some of her earlier patterns. However, this viewpoint is too limiting. Retrospectively, we can see a benefit in those channel changes: they pressed her to become aware of herself in various areas of consciousness. The rash pressed her to become aware of her body, the bolt of lightning to visualize, and the voice to listen to herself. It is conceivable that she might have cleared up her rash through simply being quicker to make changes. But healing and behavioural change are not the only goals of your process. Process awareness and the ability to perceive the world and yourself in many different ways are among the goals of channel switching and edges.

So begin again in meditation. Ask yourself: what channel am I in now? Discover the channel and amplify the events occurring there. If you notice sudden content changes or channel switches, check to see if an edge was present. Did you want to avoid something or was it too magnificent for you to believe in? If you do not easily discover an edge, then follow the switching, increase your awareness and learn about your endless capacity to know the world through different channels.

Chapter 7
ALTERED STATES

The very process which lies behind your wandering mind can also be a life-saving tool when you get stuck in a long-term meditation or reach an unresolvable point. A wandering mind is an unconscious attempt to alter a particular state. In this chapter I will discuss altering states as a useful method for working on all sorts of meditation and non-meditation problems.

When the reverse of the wandering mind happens, when your process centres and sticks to a frightening and impossible issue, you are in an inextricable situation. In analytical circles, one says that you have been taken in by a complex: hearing the same voice, seeing the same face, feeling the same sadness, again and again. Your ability to process your difficult spot is independent of the content of the complex. If you know the process structure of what is happening, you can work with yourself.

Most of the time you become stuck in one channel. And if you get stuck in the channel which you occupy least frequently, you are like a person stuck in a foreign country who cannot speak the language there. The characteristics of the channel – its language – overwhelm you. Most people do not realize their predicament and simply feel they are getting sick, going crazy or are about to die. Or, less dramatically, they may feel depressed or unable to work any longer on meditation. My recommendation is to discover your edges, find out how they structure your process, test them, go over them and, above all, learn how to *change channels*. Let me explain how to do this.

GOING CRAZY IN THE UNOCCUPIED CHANNEL

Visual types normally get lost in their chaotic, unknown and unoccupied proprioception. They are afraid that they will suffocate, that their heart will stop, or that they will become paralysed. Proprioceptive types, on the other hand, fear the insanity of monstrous visions or unbearable noises; people who are gifted in movement fear the invasion of others or the impossible statements of inner voices; and people who are good in relationships are frequently afraid of being possessed by inner scenes and voices.

CHANGING CHANNELS

Channel-changing techniques can be very useful in such situations. If you have been meditating, you know the channel you are stuck in and can change it. The simplest and most effective channel change is to translate your experience from an unoccupied channel into an occupied channel. For example, a musical person can try to hear a frightening vision, turn it into a symphony and continue to process it auditorially.

A visual person could see a movement which would otherwise terrify him. A kinaesthetic or proprioceptive person could transform an awful internal dialogue into a localized body experience such as a fight between two hands; or she could experience a difficult relationship issue in the body and work with her body to solve the relationship problems. A visual or auditory person could first feel a dreadful body symptom and then translate it into a song or a picture.

One woman was overwhelmed by fear and panic which she felt as an uncontrollable shaking in her body. She was a visual type and so I helped her by recommending that she change channels and use her visualization. She made a picture of a shaking, terrified person, and told a story about this person. This switched the process from her unoccupied proprioception into a visualization and enabled her to work with control over what was happening to her.

A man who tends to be an auditory type thought, during meditation, that he would die from his unoccupied proprioception, which was choking him in the form of an allergy attack. I pressed him to listen to his breathing and tell me what it sounded like. He heard a motor trying to get started on a cold day. That fantasy reminded him of the trouble he had been having getting started in a freezing cold relationship. While he was talking about this, his allergy attack disappeared. His process was trying to get him started in a channel which was foreign to him.

A woman had an asthma attack during meditation and feared for her life. Her attack subsided when, with encouragement, she told a story about a life and death situation. She suddenly discovered how much she wanted to do some intellectual writing before she died. She had switched from a body feeling to an auditory tale and thus could process her life and death situation usefully.

A movement-oriented man got lost in his hearing: he thought a voice would drive him crazy. He got himself out of the auditory hallucination by dancing the voice and the personality behind it. It is difficult to appreciate the process which is happening, follow its message and simultaneously give the observer-ego enough security to complete it. Changing from an unoccupied channel to an occupied one is certainly one useful way of creating this security without repressing the dreambody message.

What really happens when you switch channels? Switching transforms, translates and transmutes an unacceptable message or impossible 'language' into an acceptable one, not by changing the content but by recreating it in a language which one can 'speak'.

A surprising realization comes from this. The sometimes terrifying and impossible nature of the unconscious is due to the inability of the individual to work with the foreignness of the channel and almost never to the impossibility of the message!

THE KUNDALINI

This reminds me of a woman's dream of a terrifying snake which wanted to approach her. She woke up in shock. She began her meditation by feeling the snake in her body as uncontrollable shaking. This feeling was so unbearable, so automatic and uncontrollable, that she panicked. She courageously experienced as much of the shaking snake as she could, and then changed channels to movement – she was a dancer and her occupied channel was movement – and began choreographing the tremors in her body. Back and forth she went, from movement to the proprioceptive vibration. After half an hour of switching, the vibrations radiated throughout her entire body and she broke out into one of the most magnificent dances I have ever witnessed. The snake was her authentic dance, her dream powers coming to life, the Self which burned inside her. She had a kundalini experience, that is, the experience of being moved by an inner spirit.

THE WARRIOR'S ALLY

Castaneda's shaman, Don Juan Matus, uses an interesting and useful metaphor to describe the great complexes and disturbances in life. He speaks of 'allies' and 'shields of armour'. It is unusual for people to meet their allies during meditation, but it does happen, as in the serpent dream just mentioned. According to Don Juan, the ally is a special power, the wisdom of your unconscious, which can help you and guide you in life in a way that no human being could. During meditation the ally appears most frequently in the form of a terrifying attack such as a sudden body symptom, voice, hallucination, movement or visionary figure, or as a synchronicity.

The mythical warrior tames her ally, derives a secret from its disturbance and makes it into a partner through battling with it. According to shamanic tradition, the warrior prepares for this battle by developing her ability to confront the unknown and create shields. Switching into a main channel could be one of the 'warrior's shields' which she uses when she feels overcome. In process terms, the shamanic act of meeting the ally is expressed by meeting a strong signal or a terrifying experience occurring in an unoccupied channel. The point is not just to meet and integrate the experience, but to become familiar with the unknown channel by feeling at home in it. The warrior's way would be to switch back and forth between occupied and unoccupied channels.

TRAINING

The warrior's shield may be useful, but it does not come ready-made. It is something you need to develop *before* you run into the ally! Channel-switching techniques can be developed just as you might practise jogging to build up your physical condition.

The proprioceptive-visual switch can be practised by first feeling your inner body sensations and then making a picture out of them. If you feel tired, for instance, try to make a picture of a tired person in a certain situation and you will get the symbolic significance of your fatigue. Take the body feeling you are having now, and make a sound or movement that corresponds to it. If you are bothered by a sound or voice, can you feel it in your body? Where? Move the experience of that voice. Can you make pictures of it?

The same procedure can begin with visions. Think of a picture or scene which is difficult for you. Listen to the noises accompanying the pictures, but do not look at them; just listen. Or find a part of your body which corresponds to the picture and process it physically. You can work on your dreams in the same way. Take a dream figure or scene, associate it with a body part, and interact with it physically. I will explain this in greater detail in the next chapter.

DISTURBANCES

Most disturbances occur in unoccupied channels. Let us say you are in the midst of a yoga position and are enjoying heaven on earth, a sort of samadhi. Then a dog in the meditation room begins to bark. You have become attached to your proprioceptive experience of samadhi and detest the dog. But something new wants to happen to you. Disturbances are secondary processes which you will probably not be able to get away from. Hear the dog and switch channels, feel him in your body, make the associated movements, and you may find yourself in a state you have needed for a long time.

Altered States of Consciousness

In Chapter 2 I talked briefly about altered states. I mentioned that you have two processes, a primary and a secondary. The primary process is the one you identify yourself with, the secondary is the one which seems to happen accidentally to you, like the dog barking, or a sudden voice in your ear, or a pain in your stomach. The secondary process is often carried in the channels which you do not control or use much, or do not identify with.

For example, if you are a successful business person driving to work in the morning and are held up by an accident, your primary process is being a successful, punctual business person, and your secondary one is relaxing, slowing yourself down. The secondary one happens to you; it disturbs, surprises and annoys you. You should remember this when you are meditating; if something happens to you, if you are flexible, you can alter your state of consciousness by picking up the secondary process. Consciousness, in this conventional sense, refers to your primary process, the one you identify yourself with, and the one not wanting to be disturbed.

When you are meditating, it is usually your primary process which intends to meditate. It may be doing a good job, getting enlightened, satisfying your meditation teacher, being a better meditation student than anyone else, having a big experience, relaxing or becoming wise. Whatever your primary process is, you can recognize it by contrast with what is disturbing you.

Perhaps your disturbing secondary process is the need to fall asleep while your primary need is to meditate. Who is this in you who wants to sleep? If fatigue is a proprioception, make a picture of the feeling, and see who this person is. You may surprise yourself and awaken right away.

A Fun Meditation

Primary and secondary processes, as such, change in time, and may even change in the course of five minutes. If in meditation you find yourself rigidly holding on to your primary process, then do so, but notice how you do it. Hold on consciously, not letting anything in. Notice how your muscles work to do it and make a picture of the muscle experience.

Create your primary process deliberately. Notice which channels you use to do this and which you keep out. This could be a lot of fun. Now, knowing your primary process, use your unoccupied channels to alter states. You can do this any time, while sitting with people, while driving, or while meditating alone. Everything — is meditation for a meditator.

What actually happens when you alter states? Your focus or consciousness is changed and has illuminated a secondary process to which you had previously not paid attention. Nothing but your focus has been changed. In meditation, you work on becoming aware of your focus, broadening it, making it more tolerant and more able to deal with life and its disturbances.

For example, right now I am identified with talking to you. I hear myself talking while I am writing to you. And at the same time, I notice that this primary process is being disturbed by a secondary one: Barbara comes in from outside because she wants to work indoors. As far as I am concerned, my body feels like running on the beach. I think it must be time to alter my own consciousness, to switch channels, to move – so I will see you again soon. I am going to change channels and identities. Bye.

SUFFERING

All forms of suffering share at least one common characteristic. The sufferer is a victim of a thing or person creating the suffering, an evil persecutor. Individuals deal very differently with suffering. Dying people, to begin with at least, fight their fate. Later they may have dreams and body experiences which make them join it and stop fighting against their suffering.

It is very unusual for people to want consciously to sympathize or identify with the part of themselves causing their suffering. Everyone tends to stay with the primary process: they hate the persecutor. Yet, unconsciously, of course, each person becomes the persecutor and then suffers without even knowing why.

NOT BEING ABLE TO MEDITATE

As long as you unconsciously identify with the sufferer and remain unaware of the pain creator, you have the feeling of being stuck. This factor and not fully experiencing the suffering are two reasons for continuous suffering. *If you are unable to meditate, you have lost the position of the all-important metacommunicator who can work on the total process, and have identified with one part of the persecutor-victim drama* (see illustration 14).

Many people who suffer a great deal say they cannot meditate. Their problem is that they identify themselves with being the victims of a pain creator and they deal with this by avoiding it. Why is it that a simple channel change like telling a story about a suffering person helps these people so much? From the process viewpoint the reason is simple. They feel better because they have switched identities. They are no longer identified as sufferers, but have become fair observers, creators, tellers of a story. The earlier suffering was due to their unconsciousness.

Jung often said that a way of reducing suffering is to find the meaning in a difficult event. Finding meaning reduces suffering by discovering its purpose. The same holds true for finding the

14 *The Nightmare* by John Henry Fuseli

metacommunicator or objective observer who stands outside of the persecutor-victim drama. If you are identified with only one part of yourself, then there is no metacommunicator, no one is there to work with this part. You cannot decide to investigate it further, to amplify it, or even amplify the suffering because you are it. One of the reasons for working on yourself is to develop a relationship to many aspects of yourself and to be able to get into them and let them unfold.

The more you work on yourself, the less you will identify with only one part, and the more you will metacommunicate. Thus, even if you are submerged in some difficult piece of fate, you remember the possibility of *changing channels and switching identities* and can go deeper into the message and story of suffering. For example, you may feel miserable and yet be able to make a picture of someone who is suffering and tell yourself a story about this person. I think the greatest gift of meditation is that it operates automatically, continuing unabated in all states of being – wakefulness, sleep or even coma.

AN EXAMPLE OF ILLNESS

When someone is sick, they may dream that they are well or experience moments of well-being in their meditation. This is possible because, like any other process, physical pain occurs to only part of the personality. When the sufferer meditates, the creator of suffering appears as a part of the body, as a dream figure or as a spirit. This part, 'the disease-maker', does *not* feel pain. If you switch and work with the pain-maker instead of only with the primary process, the victim, then you can work with your own illness, amplifying your symptoms and investigating their significance. They frequently disappear as they acquire meaning.

This reminds me of a woman in one of my seminars who had a very painful sore throat. At first she just lay around, suffering from fever and exhaustion. She suddenly remembered that she could meditate and decided to be very exact about her pain. She felt her sore throat to be like an ice-cold, sharp piece of metal. This was a channel change from proprioception to visualization. She felt the pain caused by this instrument and could go no further with her process, so she decided to switch identities and she became the metallic weapon. The message of the weapon was, 'You are too nice and too soft! Get up and stop being so frightened of voicing your opinions!' To my surprise, she integrated this message by conflicting with the voice itself. She got hard and metallic with it and decided to write her opinions and not express them verbally. Her sore throat immediately disappeared.

SUFFERING IN RELATIONSHIP

One of the central experiences in relationship difficulty is that you are the victim of someone else who is mean to you, who has betrayed you, or who has coldly abandoned you. The other person becomes the secondary process. If you have severe relationship problems, then you are pressed to think about, hate, love, miss or avoid the other person all the time, outside and inside your fantasies. Working introvertedly on these problems in meditation can give you great relief. One method is to feel like the victim while the other person is your persecutor. This is what you do all the time, but now you are doing it deliberately and with awareness. An alternative is to switch identities and attempt to be the secondary process pressing you to go through deep suffering.

Identifying with the other side of a relationship problem makes you a mixture of your primary and secondary processes. I strongly recommend trying this because if you do not, you will unconsciously become the evil one towards yourself or others, and this is less constructive than doing it consciously.

Let me tell you an amusing story. During the summer I had to see many people. I began to feel like a victim of the public. I was finally able to find some peace and solitude by hiding out in this beach house, and then suddenly there was a banging at my door this morning. 'Damn it,' I thought, 'there is no telephone and no post-box, how could anyone find me here?' In walked a long-lost friend. I was infuriated. Why, then, hours later, when I finally asked this person to go, was I smiling?

Later I meditated on this and found myself focusing mischievously upon Barbara who was meditating. I felt like a trickster and decided to disturb her. She now became my victim and I was the evil one! She got upset and told me to be quiet. I sat in meditation again and the trickster reappeared and said, 'You jerk, you shouldn't apologize for me but integrate me. I was the one in you who smiled when your long-lost friend left because I enjoyed her coming. She, like me, is a disturber of the peace! It's fun to make trouble, try it!'

Chapter 8

DREAM AND BODY WORK ALONE

Last night I dreamed that a woman gave me a beautiful, ancient Chinese lantern. It was a little thing about the size of a hand, long and square, with tiny ornamental paintings on it. And this little lantern was meant, of all things, to hang over the telephone and teapot in my office. I use my teapot a lot when working. I love to drink tea, both alone and with my clients.

Awake now, I think it was a beautiful dream, but what does it mean? What do I associate with my telephone? I don't like it! It rings all the time and I can't deal with it. Instead of hiring a full-time secretary, I bought an answering machine. And my teapot? I really love my teapot. Oh, that teapot has been the source of many inspiring contacts with other human beings. It is a real ritual, satisfying and relaxing, to share tea with someone. Sometimes I even fantasize about a Zen tea drinker who makes an art of drinking tea.

What could this dream have to do with me? I have just disappeared for the week into the mountains to get away from my telephone and I am completely alone. Does the dream mean I should have more eros in my relationships or in my work? My intellectual guesses sound right but do not satisfy me.

Since I am in a meditating mood, I will leave my computer and take a walk. I intend to let go of what I am doing, and to examine my *dreaming process*. My theory is that to understand a dream fully you have to feel your own dreaming process. So I begin and find myself looking outside, enjoying the sun as it beams through the blue sky and illuminates the snow-covered peaks. I am sitting down and enjoying just looking. I love being here.

Bang! The meaning of the dream now becomes clear to me as a pictorial representation of the process I am experiencing. The dream means what it portrays: a Chinese lantern, the illumination of the Chinese way, the Tao, rules my telephone, my communications. Right now, the dream has to do with my writing; expresses my contact with you, the reader.

When I am writing this book, I often get tired. I should take a walk, enjoy the mountains, and then come back and talk to you some more. But no, I have an edge. I tend to stay on the phone too long, feeling bad for someone who needs help and acting as if I had the energy to give it. Finally I end up feeling like a suffering victim of public abuse! My primary process is to be helpful; my secondary, to be a Taoist and follow my fatigue.

PARADIGMS IN DREAM AND BODY WORK

The paradigm implicit in the dream work above, and which I follow in working with dreams or body problems, is that I do not know what 'dream' or 'body' means. Thus, when someone tells me a dream, I think to myself that the word 'dream' is a general term meaning no more than an experience happening to a sleeping person. So I listen and look and feel in order to find out what the individual in front of me means by the word 'dream'.

I keep my theories to a minimum. I do not think that the dream is a compensation, though most are; nor that it is a process trying to happen, though most are; nor that it represses sex, though many do; nor that it is something trying to happen in the here and now, though many are; nor that it is the royal road to the unconscious, because the body is royal too; nor that it should be associated to, though this is what many people need to do; nor that it should be acted out, though many do this spontaneously; nor that it is a message from another world, though many dreams turn out to be just that.

I do not deal with dreams. I deal with the dreaming processes. Thus, I hold that I have no dream theory. The method which has proved most exciting, useful and practical in everyday work with dreams is to follow the unknown. The most positive feedback from my clients follows when I forget the words 'dream', 'body', 'pain', 'issue' or any other term which I do not fully understand, and seek the exact process happening in front of me. Thus, I work with a process paradigm and not with a given dream concept, because such a concept usually leaves out the body, the living, momentary unconscious.

I arrived at the process concept some years ago after writing *Dreambody*. I had come to a personal impasse. I had written *Dreambody* using the paradigm of analytical psychology, but I could no longer fit my results into the format of analytical thinking. It was as if I had been sailing far out at sea in a leaky boat.[1] I kept patching it up until I came to the crisis point. If I designed another boat, I might run into trouble with some of the original boat builders. But I realized that the time and energy I had been putting into patching up the old boat could be invested in building a new one. With the new boat I could sail out to sea, maybe even further than before. So, with some sadness, fear and excitement, I began to build another boat, the one you and I are now sailing in. Its construction is based upon the earlier model, though it seems to sail as if it had no history. Thus, I always refer with love to Jung, for it is really he who has given me the idea that dreams are their own solutions. Processes are self-explanatory.

INDIVIDUAL DREAM WORK

If you follow the process of individual dreamers, you will notice that some automatically begin to associate when telling a dream. Associations should be used with such people. Others will automatically begin to dialogue with a figure in their dream; thus, Gestalt techniques or active imagination are the methods which they have for working on their dreams. Other people will forget the dream right away and enter into another topic. Some will gesture wildly when they get to a certain section of the dream; movement work would be well suited to them. Each client has his or her own dream work. Dreams are processes trying to happen.

A process worker need not be familiar with the many different techniques available for dream work. Theoretically, you should be able to derive the required form of dream work from the individual dreamer. You have to be wide awake to do that. You have to work on a dream and then watch for the client's feedback.

A unifying process paradigm pulls together the various schools of psychology, so that dream and body work, meditation and healing, vision quests and medicine, have more relationship to each other than ever before. It also ties together various individual experiences, such as body problems, relationship difficulties, dreams and fantasies.

AN EXAMPLE

A man has worked his whole life as a caretaker. He comes to see me because of heart problems. But when he sees me he forgets his heart pain and tells me the following dream: 'I dreamed that *people broke into my home*. They were *drunk* and pushed me around. They took over my house and then just sat around relaxing.' As he told me this dream, he put his hand on his chest when he said they '*broke in*'. I asked him what part of his body his 'home' was in. After a while, and apparently without remembering that he had put his hand on his chest, he said, 'My heart.'

Then I asked him what part of his body the *drunks* were in. He said they were in his arms. He spontaneously told me that recently, during his work, he had become exhausted and lost all the energy in his arms. He was fed up with serving people and being a caretaker. He constantly got into fights with his boss. He wanted a new life. 'But,' he said, 'I must go back to work.' As he said this, he put his hand back on his chest. I asked him what he felt and he said, 'My heart pain just came back.' 'Let in the drunks,' I said. His heart pain increases when he pushes himself to work if he really doesn't want to. 'Letting in the drunks' means allowing the minority part of him to take over temporarily: relaxing and not working so hard for others.

The drunks in his dream break into his heart as they do into his living room in the dream. His exhaustion with being a caretaker in life appears in his arms. Trying to keep out the drunks gives him heart trouble. He understood his dream immediately because he experienced his heart trouble in connection with feelings about work. The dream work touched his body and made him feel better.

THE EFFECTS OF PARADIGMS

If we had looked at his dream from the viewpoint of compensation, we would have understood an aspect of his psychology. However, because a paradigm organizes your observations, it is possible that we might not then have seen his hand on his heart. If we had thought the dream represented a repression of a childhood problem not yet worked out, then we might have been able to discuss his difficulties at work as if they were unresolved parental problems, but we might have missed his fear of an immediate death. If we had asked him to act out the different figures of the dream and he had said he couldn't, then we would have started a fight to bring up the father problem. Each paradigm or belief fits a certain moment; hence, each is correct and necessary, but may not be sufficiently adapted to a given client.

WORKING ALONE

Step 1 The Paradigm

I discuss paradigms in great detail because they strongly influence the way you deal with yourself when you are alone. If you are not able to work on your dreams, then you might consider 'how' you are working on yourself, instead of feeling guilty because you cannot work on yourself alone. What is your present belief about how to work with yourself? What paradigm are you following? What is your method? Write it down. Is it your own private mixture, is it based on association, acting out, active imagination, interpretation of repressions or visualization?

Step 2 Alone or not Alone?

The second step is to decide whether or not you want to work on your material alone. Working with others may help with a problem you are fooling yourself about. Working with someone else, however, brings in relationship issues, and it may be difficult, for one reason or another, to find someone who will be able to follow your individual, internal process. In this case, you would probably decide to continue alone.

Step 3 The Write-Up

Write down your edges, the weird dreams you have been having, the body problems which interest you, the relationship difficulties and synchronicities which have happened to you, your professional situation, etc. Then write down your present focus. Do you want a solution to a problem? Do you want to know more about yourself? Or do you need more energy?

Step 4 Follow the Process

Meditate. Follow your process as it moves around in different channels and write down the results of your meditation. Catch what happens to you, and check on the relationship between the result and what you had in mind when you began the meditation. You will notice that *your meditation mirrors and completes the unfinished scenes in your dream.*

Step 5 Edges, Channels and Changing Identity

After doing this work, you may feel complete and finished. If, however, you understand your dream and body problem but are still unsatisfied, then consider one of the following possibilities which frequently lie behind meditation problems.

Edges Investigate your edges. Write them down and find out how they organize your dreams and body problems. In the example above, the caretaker's edge was just to relax and stop caring for people.

Change Channels Change the channels in which you have been working. If you were working visually, try movement; move with the experiences you had been seeing. If you have been moving, sit down and write out a dialogue with yourself.

If you have been working on a body problem, and are not satisfied with the resulting process, then I suggest that you paint it.[2] Feel your body and then draw the outline of the body you have been feeling. Next, spontaneously paint into that outline whatever you think is there (see illustration 15). Now follow the artistic process. If a part of the painting attracts you for some reason, amplify it by enlarging it, or draw it in greater detail. If the same colour has been used in different parts of your body painting, it is an indication that these parts are related in the same process. Try using this colour spontaneously, letting anything come out of the colour, in order to find out what it is trying to express.

Victim Identification Check out whether you are possessed by one identity. If you identify as a victim and are splitting off the persecutor, be careful about who might be working on your dream. If it is the persecutor, then your inner work will hurt you; you are not working on your parts, a part is working on you. This very discovery may be your dream process.

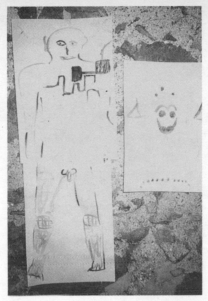

15 Body painting of pain in a man's elbow

BODY CHANNELS IN DREAM WORK

A dream can be understood in greater detail by translating it into a body channel. As I write this I begin to think of my dream about the Chinese lantern. Now I am interested in how the dream relates to my body. So I ask myself where I feel the Chinese lantern in my body. After a few minutes, I feel it in my head, between my ears. Now, in half meditation, I ask myself where I feel the telephone in my body . . . in my throat. Where is the teapot? In my heart.

Now I understand my dream physically. My throat has been feeling dry, but I thought it was due to the altitude and the cold mountain temperatures. I have also been feeling lots of strength and pressure in my chest, which makes me take deep breaths. My head feels well, no headaches, no colds, a lot of alertness. So my body work consists of what is happening right now. Putting the lantern over the telephone and teapot means letting the alertness govern my throat: I need to stop talking before I dry up. Time to go skiing. Try your own dream work now.

PART III
WORLD WORK

Chapter 9

RELATIONSHIP WORK

Relationship is not normally an object of meditation. Thus, many meditation procedures are supplemented with special oaths such as the famous Bodhisattva vow which ensures that after achieving enlightenment the meditator remains on the human plane for the benefit of other people (see Trungpa 1984). According to Buddhist tradition, the initiate pledges that he will not go into samadhi but will stay here for others and help them until they too can leave with him in the direction of freedom.

There is a beautiful story exemplifying this pledge.[1] A wise and enlightened Indian king once dreamed that his people would be poisoned and driven mad by evil rains. He warned his people about the coming catastrophe, but to no avail. When the rains came, everyone drank and went crazy, as predicted in his dream. So what did he do? He drank the water as well in order to be with them, and he went crazy too.

This story about the courageous king is a metaphor for those who want to leave this world, who have become depressed and tired of its madness and cannot see the purpose of living any longer. There is, however, a subtler message to the story. This king was not simply courageous; he was also one-sided. He may have been enlightened as long as he was a king, but not as an ordinary man. He therefore had to go back to ordinary, everyday life to become enlightened there as well.

For the king to leave enlightenment he needed consciously to experience how crazy he became when he encountered everyday problems such as earning money, caring for the kids, shopping in a crowded store and staying in the joy and tension of relationships.

The king's decision to drink the poison is the decision to enter samsara, the whirlpool of this world. It is frightening and important to realize that the king's enlightenment does *not* free him from worldly insanity. Real enlightenment means entering this world and becoming as crazy as the rest of us! Many spiritual leaders cannot help us with worldly problems because they have not sufficiently experienced their own worldly madness. Hurrah for the Indian king!

Either you voluntarily take the vow of the Bodhisattva and remain here to help others, or else you will be forced despite yourself to become a Bodhisattva. The world may depress you, you may want to leave your body and this planet, you may not want to drink the insanity of this earth, but most of us have no choice; we have to do these things. We all have to breathe the air and drink the acid rain. We all have to live in the tension of war.

Don Juan would say that the world is just perfect for the spiritual warrior interested in becoming himself. A realistic enlightenment today is a political activity; it entails a relationship with both the immediate and the distant environment. This chapter will focus upon relationship processes with the immediate environment and the next chapter upon global processes.

THE IMMEDIATE ENVIRONMENT: THE RELATIONSHIP
CHANNEL

You are in a relationship channel when you continually fantasize about someone else and cannot integrate his or her behaviour or find it in yourself. You are in the relationship channel if you cannot avoid thinking about, loving, hating or identifying with another human being. You are always in relationship to something. The experiences you have when you are meditating alone can be understood as part of your response to the world or to the universe. When you are with another person, your reactions can be understood as part of your connection with that person.

INTRODUCTED WORK

If there is no possibility of working on a relationship problem with the other person because he or she is not around, cannot be reached, or does not want to work on the relationship with you, then your process is to deal with the relationship alone. In this case, you have many choices, some of which I have mentioned earlier.

The introverted way is to understand the relationship problem as if it were a part of you. In this case, the other person or people are secondary processes which are bothering you. Meditation work on relationship can proceed by simply noticing what your process is trying to bring you, by carefully following your channel experiences, and by allowing your process to find its own solution to the problems.

A shorter, more direct method of alleviating the suffering is to look at, listen to or feel the other person, and meditatively ask yourself how you are like him or her; or you might imagine the difficulty you are having with this person, and watch your own behaviour in relationship. Ask yourself what edge you have with this person. How are you unfree, what keeps you from following your instincts and impulses with this person?

Another useful method of working introvertedly with relationships is to see the other person, or people, feel them in your body, notice their movements, and then make a courageous leap and be them. Look like them, sound like them, move like them, and find out how you might need their qualities in yourself. The resulting insight will surprise you.

EXTRAVERTED WORK

If it is possible to work on the relationship with the other person, then I would advise you to do so, and also to study yourself simultaneously; watch for your own signals and use your eyes and ears to observe the other person. Many relationship problems can be solved rapidly by picking up and processing the other person's conscious and unconscious messages, namely their double signals. I deal with this in great detail elsewhere (see pp. 105–6). For a comprehensive look into relationship work, see my *The Dreambody in Relationships*.

The following recommended procedure for working on relationship problems with another person is a blend of relationship theory and meditation practice. The philosophy of this method is that one partner alone can neither win nor lose a relationship conflict: either both lose or both win. And the best way to win a relationship conflict is to make discoveries about yourself. This relationship work can be used at any time, but is especially useful with those who are not verbally oriented or who consented only doubtfully to work on the relationship. It is useful with little children, with highly disturbed people, or when one is blocked in any interpersonal situation.

Pause First

Sit with the person or people you want to do relationship work with and state your side of the problem, then ask them to state theirs. After they have finished talking, do not react, but pause and meditate upon your reactions to their statements. Instead of simply reacting verbally, directly and unconsciously as you normally do, take the time to notice what is happening within yourself. Stop. Tell the other person that you are pausing not to drop out but to study yourself. This in itself will greatly relieve most relationship issues.

Feel and See

Consider a situation in which someone makes you angry. Stop and feel what is happening in yourself; use your proprioception. Do not talk about it, but feel it for yourself first. Pause, feel it and now amplify your feeling. Is your heart beating quickly, is your blood pressure rising, do you have hot flushes on the back of your neck, do you feel like running away, like killing someone?

Now switch channels while conserving the process. Feel whatever you are feeling in your body, and then make a picture out of these feelings. Make certain that your vision is a picture of what you are feeling and not an avoidance of your emotions. Do not avoid the emotional insanity of this planet! If you are feeling rage and then see a bird flying in the sky, you have not only switched channels, but you have also switched processes! You have substituted or repressed your anger, for the bird does not contain the same intensity of emotion as the feeling of rage. Be careful. Do not simply block out your emotion or anger. A vision of a grizzly bear eating someone up is a more convincing channel change because it conserves the process.

Expose and Interact with Your Madness

The next step is for you to interact with the image of your proprioception. I strongly recommend that you do this out loud so that your partner can hear and see you doing this. In this way, a part of the relationship which had been experienced only implicitly between the two of you becomes externalized as part of the communication system. If you don't bring this figure up and out or work with it consciously, you will become unconsciously identified with it. Identifying unconsciously with a part means behaving with your partner as if in a dream. This perpetuates a vicious circle, and continuing it is unnecessarily painful.

A man once came to one of my seminars. He had been in jail because of his uncontrolled anger, and had just been released. As soon as he saw me he immediately flew into what I thought was a paranoid rage, accusing me of things I could not possibly have done. After trying unsuccessfully to solve the conflict directly, I noticed that I was inwardly putting him down by thinking he was psychotic. I decided to go internal, to pause, feel and see what was happening in me. I felt my heart racing and my body sweating profusely. I stayed a moment with these inner proprioceptions and

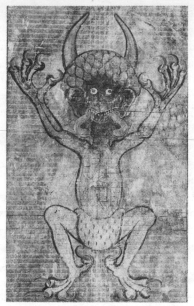

16 Red-headed devil

when I felt that I had amplified them enough, I switched channels and made a picture out of them. There, to my chagrin, I saw a red-headed woman raging around, banging on the walls of her room, crying out that she had been wronged (see illustration 16). I talked to her out loud, in front of the man.

'My dear red-headed devil,' I said to her, 'you are flipped out yourself but claiming that the other is crazy. I don't understand why you are so quick-tempered. Are you enraged because you are hopeless and afraid that this man is not going to change? Maybe he'll change or maybe he won't. The gods have sometimes been known to accomplish things no one else could. Give this man a chance.'

Before I had the chance to check out what effect this dialogue had on the inner figure, the man broke down and cried. He said that no one had ever given him a chance or believed in him. We

104

both wept, and the communication block between us was dissolved in tears. We were then able to sit down and talk about the problems at hand. We both won the battle; he felt understood, and I discovered my own red-headed devil.

Creating Dream Figures

You can observe how such inner figures can be created if you work internally with your reactions. If you are meditating and someone starts to talk to you, you become infuriated or disturbed. If you do not pick up your disturbance, you will split it off and it will reappear in a dream. I remember, for example, a phase in my life when I was meditating often and trying to stay very cool. One day my daughter came by to play with me. I acted sweetly to her, but when I closed my eyes I saw the reaction I had split off, not wanting to have it: a figure of a nasty man. I brought him out and acted like him, making a game with her out of my meditation figure. Meditating and working internally in the real world requires this kind of awareness.

Double Signals

These split-off dream figures are parts of yourself which you need to find out more about and which need to be brought into life. They appear regularly in your dreams and in your communication with the environment. These 'double signals' are part of the confusing messages we send. A double signal is an unconscious body gesture which expresses the inner dream figures you do not identify with. For example, my disturbance with my daughter must have been expressed by my cheeks turning red or my breathing becoming more rapid. If I had amplified these proprioceptions, I would have arrived at the same information that was carried in the vision of the nasty man.

If you work internally with yourself, you need little help to discover your own unconscious body gestures and the proprioceptive feelings they arise from. Process-oriented meditation makes it easier to get in touch with your own dreambody in relationships.

The mechanics of double signals in communication are as follows. The dreambody expresses itself in many channels at once. A visual dream figure can appear in your proprioception or in a body motion. As a result, you make some gesture, like an angry frown or a quick and violent hand motion, that can be traced to your dreams and symptoms. These gestures, like the dream figures associated with them, are archetypal, and the result is that people mistakenly believe that they understand them. Everyone unconsciously picks up these rapid movements and usually misinterprets them. Thus, double signals are your dream figures, secondary processes picked up in your body gestures by those around you.

Your partners react to these signals without knowing it. They may get angry at you without even knowing why. If your partner gets angry without knowing it, chances are you will get angry too, though you may both deny it. The result is that you both start yelling at each other that you are not angry! This is what I call a 'noodle soup'.

The moral of the story is that you should become more aware of your double signals and bring them into communication more consciously and constructively. One way to do this is to try the following exercise. Though it is out of context, it still gives you an idea of how to handle double signals when the situation arises.

Relationship Experiment

Ask a friend to tell you something which he has been keeping from you, something he likes or dislikes about you. Then, instead of interacting as you normally do, try meditating on your reactions and interacting with them yourself in the presence of your partner.

A funny example comes to mind of watching this exercise in a meditation seminar. A man told a woman he really liked her a lot and, instead of interacting as she normally would, she went internal and felt her body reactions. All she could feel was her heart, getting bigger and bigger. She made a picture of this big heart and suddenly saw a valentine card on which was written, 'Thank you for loving me. You have now become a part of my heart.' So she said to her admirer, 'This is too sentimental, but thank you for loving me. You are now part of my heart.' She had an edge against admitting that she loved being loved.

I think of meditation work on relationships as a collective clean-up. You begin to clean up some of the pollution bothering the city; you consciously process what is going on inside you and others rather than simply unleashing it on the collective.

BODY CONTACT MEDITATION

The above meditation work involves verbal interaction, visual apprehension of the other person, and proprioceptive contact with yourself. Such meditation work is well suited to most interactions in our culture. But it also avoids body contact in relationship. Body contact meditations can be a new form of connecting to people you are not familiar with, and also an important channel for understanding your present intimate relationships.

Touch your partner's hand or back and meditate. Touching with hands is usually accepted by others. Any part of the body can be used. The important thing is that the touching is mutual; both do the touching in the relationship. Touching is the beginning of a proprioceptive relationship meditation. Discover the proprioceptive signals in your back, feet, stomach, head, hands and chest. Feel what occurs.

Verbalizing your experiences as you feel them may stop them. Wait until they end naturally before talking. Let them unfold if possible by entering into movement, seeing, hearing and feeling whatever happens. You may develop a spontaneous slow massage, or leave the contact with your partner and create an authentic dance. Perhaps movement improvisation will ensue. Meditate while in movement. Move together and move slowly. You should try this with someone you like and with someone you dislike.

The results of silent, touching meditation are likely to surprise

17 Yoni, female genital

you. Many people discover deep unfamiliar feelings they have never realized before. Some find themselves disgusted by people they thought they liked, others discover subtle mixtures of dance, bonding, sexual feelings, love and hatred.

TWO PEOPLE, ONE BODY

People frequently discover afterwards that they have had the same fantasies. Proprioceptive relationship meditation is an experiment with the collective unconscious. When one woman put her finger on another's back and remained quiet, she suddenly visualized a clitoris. Her partner simultaneously saw a clitoris. There was no verbal interaction. This couple discovered a shared dream, the goddess Shakti, the yoni (see illustration 17).

Where do these simultaneous fantasies come from? Are they coincidental? In dance, one can see how two people create a dream. But in touch without movement, it is an invisible process. Since these common visions stem from body experiences, that is, touching and moving, we have to suspect that people share one and the same body!

FIELDS AND DREAMS

If the meditators' experiences are slightly different, we have the case of one dreambody having several parts. Such a 'relationship body', or global dreambody, is like our normal body, full of parts and incongruities. This experiment shows that in relationship you are part of an emotional field structured by dreamlike symbols. This is Jung's collective unconscious in practice. If an entire group sits together in a circle touching one another, the resulting experiences of the individuals can be assembled to describe the group field.

Proprioceptive relationship experiences are practised by Tantric and Taoist yogis They move and feel, love and interact meditatively, unravelling relationship mysteries which are difficult to verbalize. Such people have the chance to understand the global dreambody through direct experience, changing some of the madness of this world into meaningful relationships.

Chapter 10

EARTH WORK

When people consider the entire world, they usually think only of its inhabitants; yet the earth consists not only of people, but trees, mountains, stones, rivers, the sky and stars as well. The earth itself is actually an idea found throughout history and mythology. It was once thought that the earth was a great and unlimited power which could heal or destroy, a power which could care for everything. Many Third World or non-industrial people still see the earth as a god which informs them how to live properly.

The westerner sees the earth today as an ailing being, choked with wastes and poisons, barely able to house its overpopulated areas, full of tension and ready to explode at any moment. A very recent idea of the earth is that it is a neural network of interconnections of 'Gaia', a living anthropos (see Mindell, *The Year I*, 1985). In some traditions we must become the universal spirit of the globe.

EXPERIMENTS WITH THE EARTH

Rediscovering the earth means using our senses, not just our old ideas about the planet. The following experiment will give us personal information about the earth. Now that you have developed your proprioception, put your hands on the earth. Sit outdoors and put your hands on a piece of the earth. Meditate in this position and note what happens to you.

You may be surprised to find that your experience of the earth in this experimental meditation is very different from the informa-

18 The original earth

tion you may have read in the newspaper. Meditating on the earth
gives you a sense of her inexhaustible generosity and abundance and
her truly endless patience. The old earth is still yours, full of power,
telling you things no human being could (see illustration 18).

If you are in a part of the world where the city does not totally
obliterate the earth, open your eyes and stare at it. Watch what

happens to you when you look. Do you look only at things which are beautiful? If you are in the mountains, do you delight only in the peaks, the mountain underbrush, the rugged rocks? Study these things which you love. Watch how you look, notice what happens to you, and amplify your extraverted seeing. After a while you will experience what the yantra and mandala meditators hoped for; you become the mandala, you become the mountain and the river. This is the beginning of experiencing yourself as the earth.

EXPERIMENT WITH THE HATEFUL EARTH

But not the whole earth. What about the parts you do not like too much, the ugly stones, the rough areas which disturb you? How will you investigate these? If you disregard those parts of the earth you do not like, you are hurting her ecology. The parts you do not like must also be processed if the spirit of the earth is not to be cluttered with wasted information. I want to recommend an important meditation experiment to you, one which will help you process the difference between those parts of the earth you love and those you do not.

Go outside and take your time looking around for two hand-sized objects, one you like and another which you dislike. Now meditate while holding one of these objects at a time. Write down the results in your meditation journal. Writing in a journal helps you to integrate your meditations and interrupts their cyclical nature. The object you like turns out, most of the time, to be very much like the person you love or fantasize about loving. The object is a Self figure, a complete and whole personality which your process is trying to create.

For example, one woman picked up a round, soft stone. She said it was like her beloved: strong, powerful, smooth, direct and soft at the same time. She held this object and noticed what it did to her body. She, too, would like to be like this stone and is en route to becoming it.

The object you do not like is usually a part of yourself which you need and which you are splitting off. In the case of a priest who came to one of my seminars, a rusty metal ring from some motor bothered him. It represented all those things he did not like but needed to know better. The priest meditated upon this ring while holding it. He hated it, was disgusted by it, and wanted to get rid of it. At one point he even thought it would make him sick. He held on to his meditation as long as possible. He put the ring on one shoulder, then the other, and put it on his head. Suddenly, to his surprise, he became the rusty metal ring. He became all those rusty old things he had detested, things he did not want anyone to know about. After becoming these things, he felt wonderful. He let go of his proper, clean-cut mask and became dishevelled, dirty, unkempt and uncared for, but absolutely happy. When the meditation was over and he told me about his experience, he even looked a bit drunk. He said he felt like a bum. Excitedly, he remembered that in his dream the night before he saw a bum locked up in jail. He knew now that through awareness he could let the bum free!

THE CLOGGED-UP EARTH

Working with beloved and hated objects gives you a chance to work with your primary and secondary processes. No one likes the secondary earth processes, everyone tries to repress them, but repression means psychological impoverishment and trouble for the earth. The more waste we throw away, the more clogged up the earth becomes. Reprocessing junk instead of throwing it away is a psychological act which begins in meditation. Not processing our wastes is a symptom of not processing our experiences about the earth. Process your junk, don't just throw it out!

INTROVERTED POLITICS

Mystics experienced themselves as part of the earth. They believed that putting themselves in order would put the earth in order as well. They had their own introverted political and ecological technology. This was the implicit theory of the Taoist Rainmaker, the meditator who worked miracles by simply getting himself in order. Richard Wilhelm, the translator of the *I Ching*, told this story in a private correspondence with C. G. Jung.[1]

The next time you are upset about a world situation and feel that you have done as much as possible extravertedly, meditate on the two sides in conflict. I will never forget the Six-Day War between the Arabs and Israel in June 1967. I was very upset and found both the Arabs and the Israelis as figures in violent conflict within myself. At that time, they represented two opposing attitudes towards the world in me. My meditation ended with a peace treaty between the two sides. As I finished my meditation, I turned on the radio and heard that an agreement had been reached in the Middle East as well. There is reason to suspect that a lot of political work can be done on your own meditation mat.

But be careful: if you avoid taking an outer role in the world and only deal with its problems internally due to your own edges in relationship and extraversion, then your introversion is merely an escape from your total process. You should be learning to get over your fear of taking a stand in the world. If you do not work on your extraversion, your inner work will be disturbed and ineffective.

FINDING YOUR SPOT

Working on touching the ground is an excellent preparation for another more complex task in earth work: the vision quest. Finding a spot on the ground within a restricted area which is beneficial to you is the first step to this procedure.

I recall a very special spot-finding quest which I did at an old house in Aawangen, Switzerland. My seminar participants used the little yard outside the house as a hunting ground for their spots. Around and around we all went for an hour and a half, trying to find the magical spot which would make us feel well. I found a spot by looking, but unfortunately someone else wanted it too and got there first! What a shock! How would I deal with this? I worked meditatively on walking, looking and feeling. After about an hour, my body sat down on an impossible spot in the corner of the garden which was so steeply sloped that sitting comfortably was impossible. So I worked on my posturing, using my proprioception and my kinaesthesis in connection with the earth; after a while I found myself lying on the ground with my head pointing downhill and my legs raised in the air, knees bent over my forehead (see the plough asana, illustration 5b, p. 53). There I lay and I fell into an altered state of awareness because of the blood rushing to my head. Soon I slipped off into an ecstatic state of emptiness. What a spot!

SPATIAL OCCUPATION

This story is important because it strongly anchored the following learning experience in my body. *The place you occupy on this earth depends not only on your personal psychology but also on what spaces are already occupied.* If somebody had already written this book, I would not have been able to. If a plant had been on my spot, I would have had to find an alternative spot. Since someone else was in the spot I wanted, I was pressed to find another one. I found that by working on myself, I could get along with the new spot. In fact, it brought me more than I could have hoped for.

By analogy, the spot you are pressed into in this world, the physical and psychological spots, could be just the right ones for you, for they bring you a lot by forcing you to learn new ways of living and working on yourself. You may not like certain parts of the physical earth, certain relationship situations, or certain roles you are forced to play, but if you deal with them ecologically, that is, use them completely, you can turn the worst place into the best one.

115

THE WORLD CHANNEL

The vision quest is a world channel meditation, experiencing the earth as a wise guru who sends you messages through its cities, rivers, stones, stars and political conflicts. Your previous work on feeling, seeing, moving, hearing, relating to others and touching the earth are preparations for being in the world and treating it as a place for vision quests. Your process flows into the world channel when you are forced to focus on the world, when it seems to send you confusing messages, when it rejects or accepts you, or when it supports or annihilates your existence. You are in the world channel when you want to find out more about these messages or when you are interested in and ready to use the natural environment to seek visions and information and to become your whole self.

THE VISION QUEST

I have described the vision quest briefly in Chapter 3. Here, I need only remind the reader that the vision quest is the central religious experience of the American Indians and is characteristic of the way they relate to the world. Their religion involves communicating with the earth directly and asking her for what they need. The earth is the channel which informs them and gives them the necessary wisdom for living. The initiate on a quest first discusses her problems with a shaman, and then goes out into the wilderness and waits for a dream, vision or body experience. She brings this experience back to the shaman who helps her interpret it.

I recommend that you first meditate upon central questions in life which have been catching your interest, and that you begin your vision quest by writing them down. The next step is to go into nature as if you were meditating, and catch, hold and process the events which happen to you.

An informative and lovely story about the quest is found in H. Storm's *Seven Arrows* (1972). A young man wanted to know what he should do with his life and set out on a quest. When he came back several days later, he told his shaman that he had found nothing significant. The wise shaman questioned the boy until the latter finally admitted that at one point during his quest he wanted to take a nap on a cliff overlooking a beach (that is, he found his spot!) when he caught sight of a young woman on the beach. She was so beautiful that the young man masturbated with her image in mind. The wise shaman correctly connected this to the boy's original question and concluded that the boy's mission in life was to teach others about love.

This example shows that a central problem of the vision quest is proper evaluation of the experiences which happen to you. Our young man acted like a novice meditator in that he went out on his quest looking for a great vision where spirits would tell him magical things. This very intention, the search itself, was a primary process. But what happened to him was an unexpected secondary process, an important lesson. The process which was not predicted, which does not go along with your intentions, is the magical vision. If you miss one of these little visions, they will repeat themselves and reappear in another channel or at another time.

I have worked with many people on their vision quests and remember one woman who went out on a mountainside at sunset. As she set off, she was terrified of the dark shadows and ran into a tree. She was frightened by visions of men chasing her and she ran and ran. She spent the whole night on the mountain and had a thousand experiences.

She suffered from two problems. First, she was not clear enough about the question she was seeking to answer. And second, she did not pick up and hold on to the secondary processes which happened to her. Thus, the shadows of the trees and the visions of men were wasted because she did not realize that they were important.

I suspect one of the reasons vision quests among the Indians are frequently so dangerous, even fatally so, is that initiates are not sufficiently trained in meditation procedures. They cannot hold and amplify their experiences, which consequently amplify themselves endlessly, turning into nightmares, illnesses or accidents.

MY QUEST

I recently went on a vision quest. I wanted to know what I should do next with my life. So I went out one evening at sundown in the Colorado Rockies. I spent a long time tiredly dragging along near the Loveland Pass. As the sun went down, I found I had more energy and began running up a deserted mountain road. Up and up I went as the shadows of the night fell. As the blackness of a moonless night enveloped me I felt increasingly apprehensive. I thought, I am an analyst, I can only be scared by something which is very foreign to my identity. Therefore I should be cautious about the darkness and open up to it as much as possible. This thought, which had been so helpful to me in previous scary situations, did not help that night.

As I ran up the road, I imagined that something was running with me! I thought it must be the shadow of some tree. But, my God, the shadow started running in the opposite direction down the other side of the road! My initial impulse was to analyse this shadow away: 'It is a shadow of a tree or a sign post.' But then I realized that there would be no sign posts on such a deserted mountain road. Perhaps it was a real spirit! At this point my mind boggled at the possibility of a mountain shadow. I was terrified to death, but I remembered that integrating something would reduce its power. So I gathered up what courage I had left and decided to switch channels. Instead of apprehending the thing visually, I decided to use my movement. I thought if I didn't alter my identity, it would overcome me.

With all my will, I slowly walked to the other side of the road and, sweating profusely from sheer terror, jumped over to where the shadow was. I forced myself to move as it had, and ran down the hill at the point where I had last seen it. As I began to move, my run transformed itself into a dance. My feelings changed from fear to joy. A new thought came to me: I needed to trust my body wisdom and intuitions more because they wanted to write. Then, without having decided to do so, I ran all the way down the long mountain in one fell swoop.

My vision quest was done, and it must have hit the nail on the head, for since then every free moment has been taken up by a confrontation with that terrifying shadow. Even now, many weeks later, I find myself writing with great intensity about meditation. Though I identify myself as an analyst, teacher, researcher, lecturer, lover, father, man, etc., my secondary process these days is writing and studying meditation. I am tempted to call the author of this book 'The Dark Mountain Shadow'.

I am thankful for the gifts I have received in all the channels. I must admit, however, that of all these channels, the earth is now the most mysterious and important to me.

Chapter 11

WHO IS HERE?

After devoting a great deal of time and effort to working on yourself alone, you will start to discover the larger, overall process of meditation. If you follow your process for long periods of time, you will become aware of two different kinds of awareness: short-term and long-term awareness.

LONG- AND SHORT-TERM AWARENESS

Short-term awareness is channel awareness. It is awareness of temporary changes in signals and consciousness. Long-term awareness is insight into the process of awareness itself; it is being aware of who is meditating. If you ask yourself during a meditation 'Who is meditating?' the answer you get will show you that you are not the only one who uses your awareness.

For example, today I am in the mountains, wanting to tinker around in my house. It is early morning and I notice, as I awaken, that the sun is playing games with my eyesight. Only one eye is open and I notice dreamlike forms on the wood ceiling. My visions are like dreaming. I am aware that my process is visual, but I wonder for whom these dreamlike visions are meant. I roll over, consider sleeping, and notice that I am irritated from drinking so much orange juice before going to bed. Who is this irritated 'I'? I could feel my irritation and let a vision develop from my proprioception; or I could simply meditate on the koan: *Who* is irritated?

I want to sleep. But who wants to sleep and relax? Who wants to behave like everyone else? It sounds like a primary process, because

120

I know that I, the observer, tend to identify with being a normal guy who prefers to sleep. But he is in conflict with another part of me which wants to wake up and write. Conflict. My primary process wants to relax and putter around, to build some furniture, but another part wants to write. I focus on the writer and suddenly I feel something. If I do not write, then the impulse to write will disorient me and distract me from my primary process, from sleeping, relaxing and being a normal guy.

Why do I spend so much time unconscious? These last few days here in the mountains, I have been unconsciously identifying with a primary process of relaxing, building the house, worrying about people and money, etc. Remember the question I asked at the beginning? What are you doing when you are not meditating, when you are unconscious? The answer is, you are identifying with your primary process. The existence of a secondary process, of a part with which I do not identify, creates consciousness and forces me to develop my awareness into a metacommunicator.

Consciousness is an empirical term, it is something you can discover and create in meditation. It means that you are aware of your awareness, aware of your dreaming, that you know the meaning of what you will dream before you dream it.

CHARACTERISTICS OF CONSCIOUSNESS

Consciousness refers to being aware of your awareness. You know who is here and who is not here. Consciousness means knowing with whom you identify, knowing whom you keep out, and recognizing the primary and secondary processes which are available to you.

One of the characteristics of consciousness is that you are able to work with your life process. You feel 'up to it', not trampled by it. You feel like a multi-dimensional person. If you work with the conflicts between the processes, following them congruently, step by step, you will notice another aspect of consciousness: the experience of freedom. Imagine your process as a chariot pulled by a lion: freedom is neither being run over by the chariot nor being eaten by the lion. You drive the chariot and steer the lion.

World Work

Being conscious and awake is certainly one of the happiest, peak experiences of life. It is also easy to achieve. When you spend a lot of time working on yourself, working with the channels of your experience, noticing the observers in you who are meditating, you may get the feeling that the process is trying to awaken you as quickly as possible. The growth of awareness happens at a maximal rate.

In addition, becoming aware usually entails very few shocks, for these do not bring lasting awareness. They only terrify you momentarily. Awareness cannot take place at gun point; 'become aware or die' is blackmail and will only make you hate meditation. Nor does awareness present you with instant gratification, which would only make you content and lazy.

YOUR PERSONAL MYTH

The way awareness works in us is, I believe, by constantly and patiently chipping away at our lives in order to bring out our original form, visible in our childhood dream, in our personal myth. Jung found out years ago that what we call early childhood dreams and incidents are patterns governing our life-long process. If you dreamed as a child that gangsters were after you, then you may frequently feel like a good person constantly confronted by a gangster-like secondary process. Everything which happens makes you aware of the limitations of your goodness and sweetness and how it keeps out your own gangster-like drives.

Being aware, then, means being aware of not only the short-term situations in our lives, but also our personal myths, childhood dreams and memories, as well as of the observers in us who use our awareness.

WHO IS HERE?

Experiment in meditation by finding what channel you are in and who in you is perceiving the visions, sounds, movements, relationship issues and world processes in and around you. Who is the perceiver processing these signals?

Who is here? To know who is meditating, you might ask yourself, 'Who are these observations necessary for?' There are often observers in us who are convinced of the absoluteness of their observations and of their way of perceiving. All the signals you perceive and all the things you observe become relative and are meant for the observer who governs the meditation. If you can catch this, you can detach from both the observer and the observed, and laugh and wonder at both processes.

THE AWARENESS PRINCIPLE

Not only does your process bring you enlightenment and detachment, but it may do so as quickly as possible. I believe that there is something like an awareness principle, a law of awareness which states:

> The processes which you perceive, your focus, channel changes, edges, problems and illnesses are organized in such a way as to make you aware as quickly as possible of how your secondary process conflicts with your primary one.

For example, if you normally identify yourself as a busy person, always running around, completing work, and neglecting your physical comforts, you might have a secondary process of relaxing, taking care of yourself and paying attention to the most minute physical needs. The awareness principle would bring the secondary process to consciousness in a variety of ways; you would notice throughout the day dozens of tiny disturbances, all containing the same message of the secondary process. You will be constantly disturbed by neediness, and you will find yourself hoping to be cared for by others. You will become unexpectedly tired in the middle of the day and want to take a nap, and you might dream about a cat, stretching and purring.

In other words, the awareness principle ensures that only those visual, auditory, movement, proprioceptive, relationship and world processes occur to you which press you to become aware of your secondary process as quickly as possible.

Does this extreme drive towards awareness really exist? If there really is an awareness principle, then why are our dreams clothed in symbols and why do our bodies not simply make us go in the 'right' direction? The answer is that most people do not react to their dreams; they soon forget them. Others do not react to illnesses, even when their messages are clear. They either refuse to change or they become terrified and try to get rid of the illness. In other words, the intensity of the visions and dreams, body experiences, relationships and world situations is inversely proportionate to the degree to which we follow them.

The way to get a message to someone who does not believe in dreams, visions or body problems is to bring the message across in a gradual way. If it is too painful and intense, he will simply resist it. If, on the other hand, it is too mild, he will just ignore it. Some people wake up when relationships trouble them. Others react only when a great teacher tells them something. And those who are interested in neither relationships nor teachers change only when challenged by an illness.

The Relativity of Awareness

The awareness principle says not that you get maximum awareness but that you get the maximum amount of awareness that your given personality, in a given time and place, can absorb. Maximum awareness is a relative concept; it is relative to your particular situation. You may be quite aware in terms of where you are living now, but in other circumstances, families and cultures you might look very undeveloped. When working alone on yourself, you may be very enlightened. But when working with others, you may appear to be unconscious. If you live in the city, your process of awareness will be different from that of a peasant living in the mountains.

Hence, there are different kinds of awareness to develop. How far awareness can go, and whether or not there is an end to it, is for us to discover. We know only that the path to awareness is full of twirls and spirals, ups and downs, repetitions and paradoxes. The potential for becoming aware is available all the time; we merely have to tune in to it. Information about our many identities is constantly around us, waiting for us to perceive it.

DREAMBODY AWARENESS IN HISTORY

The process of gaining awareness of your total self has been described in great detail by the alchemists as cooking the *prima materia* until it turns to gold, by the Kabbalists as divine insight, by the Christian mystics as light, and by the Buddhists as atman, nirvana, and insight (see Wilbur 1982). The Chinese Taoists developed awareness by attempting to create eternal or 'diamond bodies' which were free of their real bodies. For many American Indians, awareness means becoming a seer. Jung spoke of the process of coming to consciousness as the individuation process whose goal was completeness or wholeness.[1] Ken Wilbur (1982) uses a combination of eastern mystical traditions and western psychology to show how we attempt to reach increasingly complete states of wholeness and enlightenment.

THE AVAILABILITY OF AWARENESS

These disciplines speak of awareness as a peak or religious experience, a supreme state of mind which we can and should reach. The best teachers, however, teach that these peak experiences don't describe what *will* happen, but what is going on *right now*. You can pick it up right now or you can wait until death. Awareness is here for everyone, all of the time. It is never too early and never

125

too late to begin. I have seen people pick up full awareness in their very last moments of life. A coma itself can be the door of awakening awareness. In the last moments of life people frequently ask themselves, 'Who is thinking, who is here, what is life?' Others ask these questions earlier. But the peak experience of awareness is potentially there whenever you awaken to find the channel you are in, who is meditating, and the person for whom life's signals are meant.

This last paragraph was supposed to be the end of the book. After I wrote it, I lay down on my black couch, took a nap and had an experience which seemed to be meant for the observer in me who wants to know what life is about. I was able to see the ordinary me, my double, and one of my tasks in life.

As I slept, I had the most intense vision I can ever remember. I could differentiate my dreaming body from the body lying on the couch. I saw my wife, Amy, a few feet in the air above me and said to her, 'This is a paranormal experience and I want you to know it.' She could not answer. (I called her on the telephone two minutes after I came out of this experience and she said that she had just been trying to meditate.)

Then I saw some peasants coming by in a tractor outside my house. Though my door and windows were not open, I could see them preparing for the winter season by going up on the ski lift at the end of the valley with their new machines. (Months later I discovered that a new lift had just been planned there, making these mountain peaks more accessible to others.)

It was important to me to realize that during this vision I knew that I was dreaming. I was so intensely awake that I could see me on the couch, and also the me connected to eternity. I meditated with complete awareness in the altered state of my vision. I was dreaming lucidly that my life and death are both just parts of me. The awareness of the vision gave me a special peace, too beautiful to describe.

It was difficult to return to my ordinary body. Any attempt to awaken hurt, and so I continued wakefully to explore the world. I went on like this for hours. Then I wanted to come out of this altered state but did not know how. I realized that some of your questions about meditation were the powerful forces pulling my spirit back into my body. Thank you.

Chapter 12

QUESTIONS

Process is its own solution. If you run into a problem during your meditation, you can get the solution from your own meditation experience. I want to encourage you to go back to yourself. Just begin by asking yourself what channel you are in at the moment. Amplify the signals in that channel and follow the channel changes which occur.

The following are common questions about meditation difficulties which I frequently encounter during my seminars. If you have questions which do not appear here, please send them to me, and I will try to answer them in future editions of this work. If I cannot answer the questions, I will present them as research projects. In this way, I hope that we can join together in researching meditation.

Question When I meditate, only banal things come to mind. In fact, banality bothers me all day long and in my dreams too. Can this be meditation?

Answer Meditation consists not only of becoming aware of the 'banal' disturbances, which apparently are secondary processes for you, but also of apprehending your primary process for which banality is an opposite. Who is meditating? You should find out who it is in you who is interested in getting beyond the banal.

Question I cannot concentrate on anything. Things keep happening too quickly for me to focus upon. What should I do?

Answer Your question tells me that you are suffering from working without enough discipline. What 'things' go through your head, and in which channel are they? Why not start from the beginning? Find the channel your process is in, amplify the signals in that channel, notice your edges and follow what happens. Another possibility is that the part of you that is meditating has the goal that things should go slowly. Rapidness may be important for a slow part of you .

Question I feel that nothing interesting happens to me in meditation. I must be a failure at it.

Answer If you look down upon what happens to you during meditation, you probably look down upon yourself all the time. It seems that you are identified with someone in you who hates you. *You* are not meditating; *a critic* is. If only a part meditates, you lack a metacommunicator who is aware of your parts. Thus, you become the victim of the critic. Try changing channels. How about feeling your dilemma and then making a picture out of this feeling? It might be useful to visualize a critic bothering a victim, and then work with your response to this picture.

Question Though you call disturbances secondary processes, I still hate noise and want peace from it when I meditate.

Answer So do I. I hate disturbances when I am meditating. Take your need for peace into consideration without analysing it. I recommend that you take your primary process seriously and tell the people around you to be quiet and respect your attempt to work. Try to quieten the level of noise around you. If you are still unhappy, you might consider your irritation to be an edge against being noisier yourself.

Question Frequently, when I meditate, I fear I will go crazy, especially when I have been working at it for a while.

Answer I have several responses to that. First, you might experiment with consciously driving yourself out of your mind, that is, out of your primary process. Your fear of craziness could be an indication that some secondary process is trying to surface and that you are too rigid about your identity. Another response is that you might experiment with stopping your silent meditations and go into ordinary life with your awareness. Why spend so much time alone? Another response is that you might need to learn more about channel changing. Go back in this book and study the sections on edges and altered states. Still another possibility is that great fears come up when you get to the central issues of your life. You may have arrived at one of your mythical origins. To deal with such basic patterns you need a great deal of patience and know-how from books and teachers of meditation and psychology.

A story of Muktananda comes to mind. He thought he would go crazy when a beautiful woman kept coming to him in his visions after he had taken the vow of chastity. His central myth, as far as I can see, was teaching about love. His guru helped him by convincing him that he was seeing Shakti. The guru did the right thing by reframing the problem so that it was no longer a disturbance, but the path to individuation. You too might consider the possibility that what is driving you crazy is the beginning of an untransformed urge which is going to bring you a great deal of balance and wisdom.

Question My problems cycle when I meditate and I cannot stop them. What should I do?

Answer Cycling happens because you have not given the content of the problem enough appreciation and attention. Examine your cycle and ask yourself what sort of edges are involved. If you get over the edges involved, I promise you your cycling will stop. I recently invested in my first piece of property and I spent several sleepless nights thinking about how I would pay for it. My edge was to ask for help, and when I finally asked a friend for financial support, the cycling stopped.

Question In your experience, what are the central places where people get stuck in working with themselves?

Answer One central place is in unoccupied channels. This is where everyone swims. The therapy for this would be to use a main channel as an aid.

Another central problem is that people get to an edge and lose their awareness. For example, if you are working on yourself and you begin to move, but stop without completing the movement, you have come to an edge. You have an edge against that particular movement; it is too violent, too loving, or too mystical for your primary process. If you do not catch the edge, you become blocked and lose your awareness of the process. Sometimes an edge appears in the form of an overabundance of visualizations. Visions change too rapidly when you do not believe in them or when you are not picking up their implicit information.

Another point people need help with is in completing experiences. People often feel or see something important and then just leave it. Completing a process means not just feeling or seeing it, but experiencing it in many channels and as completely as possible. Experiencing a process in a normally unoccupied channel is bound to heighten its importance. Use the very same channel changes which normally bother you as a device for completing your work.

Question When I begin a week-long meditation, I spend the first few days working on emotional complexes. Later in the week I get to transpersonal levels of experience. How do these levels connect?

Answer I shall assume that 'transpersonal' refers to states outside of your primary process, the experience you have of your everyday reality. Therefore, if you simply sit quietly or take a week off from what you are normally doing, you automatically change your primary process from everyday reality to a meditation attitude. This new attitude is 'transpersonal' in that it is devoted to non-ordinary, non-everyday things. Now a new task would be to carry this transpersonal attitude with you back to your ordinary life.

Question What is enlightenment for you?

Answer Enlightenment is a word I try not to use much because it is a state. I prefer to speak of waking up. For me, 'awakeness' is a relative term. An awake person has rapid access to and ability in working with altered states in many channels. She can propriocept, hear, see, feel, relate to the earth or to others, and know who is meditating.

An awake person can get into altered states and still metacommunicate. She can therefore process intense affects, like anger, in many different channels. She would be able to use occupied channels as tools for working with altered states and unoccupied channels. Being wide awake means that when you are in a state of peace you can recall difficulties which face you and work on them even though they may only be present weakly at that moment. When you are drunk you have access to sobriety. You can get deeply involved in body work and still retain your intellect.

If you are awake, you change according to the world within and around you. This means that you can vary your behaviour and perception of the world according to the signals it sends you; you change according to the feedback you get.

An enlightened individual could have a great deal of feeling and compassion for other human beings but would also be very detached and tough when this is called for. For me a highly awake person is capable of bringing out reactions to others in such a way that everyone benefits from them.

Question According to Muktananda, devotion to a guru gives you the spark you need to awaken. What do you think?

Answer I loved Muktananda. I cried when he died. I agree with him that enlightenment can happen through the spark, the shaktipat, of a good teacher. I remember one of his stories in which a professional and distinguished man received this shaktipat by cleaning Muktananda's bathroom. Muktananda came in one night and found him there, in a deep meditative trance! The guru's room itself blasted that professional person out of his rational primary process. But for me, this spark is just the beginning of an immense transformation. Now the true magnum opus begins in which that man's whole life will be transformed.

I have taken part in many rapid enlightenment situations in my workshops: I have seen shaktipats, experienced them myself, and heard many stories about how the spark can blast your whole world to pieces. Though I revere it, it is but one of my many meditation interests. Breakthroughs are the most memorable and dramatic meditation experiences, but are only the beginning. Breakthroughs occur partly because you have been resisting change for too long; without your ability to integrate them, however, they merely explode your concept of reality temporarily.

Question Do you think the world's consciousness is improving? If the awareness principle implies that life is organized in such a way that it brings us as rapidly as possible to consciousness, then wouldn't the entire world be striving for this state of awareness?

Answer I hope so. Ecological and military dangers have just awakened the world to the fact that it exists as a single unit. Genetic engineering allows us to control life, a nuclear bomb to destroy all of existence. Everything we now do must be done with great awareness or we will all be gone. These dangers are – or could be – the powerful motivation for awareness. Will the world now develop the ability to process its awareness? It has no choice.

Question   In India a religious experience is measured by three or more characteristics. It must be validated by a guru, it has to be found in the scriptures, and has to have been felt by the meditator. Do you think this is authoritarian?

Answer   Not really. You must remember that the Indian system needs these rules because it does not have a relationship channel in meditation. Its model is the detached, centred, loving individual. Without awareness of or interest in discord from others, you can easily become identified with a particular part of your process and think you are Jesus or Hitler. Therefore, many meditators just flip out and have exciting, freaky or even psychotic episodes. In such cases, the teacher and scriptures are the student's secondary process which keeps him or her from flying away into the clouds.

If you are meditating, however, in a paradigm which considers relationship an object of study, then you do not need these ancient rituals. If you identify as a religious figure, you will run into a lot of trouble in your relationships. Your relationships are a safeguard; they will press you to explain yourself, to account for your religious states. Thus, your teacher may be the scriptures, your next-door neighbour or your partner.

Question   Meditators have always claimed supernatural powers such as telepathy. Have you come across these powers in your work?

Answer   Yes, with and without meditation. 'Paranormal' events and synchronicities in the process paradigm are expressions of unknown information in the world channel. The world channel often gets filled with mysterious and remarkable events when one is about to enter into the world and in need of greater contact with spiritual and 'paranormal' forces.

Question Do you think it is important for a therapist to help clients to meditate?

Answer Yes. If you have been assuming the role of helper and healer it will be useful for many of your clients to find out how to help themselves. Most clients need help and companionship and also encouragement to appreciate the wisdom of their own processes. You might try to assist your clients in their inner work by pointing out their edges, and main and unoccupied channels, and who is meditating.

Question When I leave meditation, the world comes back to me and I get depressed. Re-entering the world after meditation is often a difficult and painful project made possible only by my love for people.

Answer I am touched by your love for others. If your feelings for people make life worthwhile, then these feelings might motivate you to focus your meditation on relationship. Then, in the process paradigm, you are still in the same meditation centre as before, you are still working on yourself alone, with or without others.

You can never really leave process-oriented meditation. For when you leave your introverted work you enter another meditation, your everyday life. Thinking that you 're-enter the world' is an illusion, because, paradoxically enough, you can never really leave it. From the viewpoint of the awake meditator, all of the many separate worlds, whether they are inner or outer, death or life, physical or mental, are all aspects of the same mysterious universe; all are different channels full of luminous signals and meaningful information waiting to be apprehended and unfolded by you.

NOTES

1 MEDITATION PROBLEMS

1. This story, originally told by Ram Dass, may be found in his 'An Encounter with Fritz Perls' in Jack Downing (1976).
2. See my *Coma: Key to Awakening* (1989) for a discussion of working with dying people and *City Shadows* (1988) for psychiatric interventions with people in catatonic states.
3. Some of the masters themselves may have these problems as well; see Bodian (1986).

2 PARADIGM SHIFTS IN MEDITATION

1. Castaneda, *Journey to Ixtlan* (1972). Trungpa (1984).

3 CHANNELS AND MEDITATION RITUALS

1. The best explanation of active imagination can be found in Hannah (1981).
2. An excellent introduction to the vision quest can be found in Storm (1972).

4 CHANNEL PERCEPTION

1. Don Juan is the name of the Yaqui Indian who was the shaman/mentor in the series of books by Carlos Castaneda. In particular, see *Journey to Ixtlan*.

8 Dream and Body Work Alone

1. I am grateful to Jim Beggs for this analogy, which can be found in Weinhold and Beggs (1984), p. 23.
2. This idea of using painting in body work was suggested to me by Rhoda Isaacs.

9 Relationship Work

1. This story is told in Trungpa (1984), p. 123.

10 Earth Work

1. See Richard Wilhelm, in a letter to Jung, Jung (1956), p. 604n.

11 Who is Here?

1. For a description of the individuation process see Jung (1944).

BIBLIOGRAPHY

Adair, Margo, *Working Inside Out, Tools for Change: Applied Meditation for Intuitive Problem Solving*, Berkeley, Wingbow, 1984.

Bodian, Stephan, 'Baba Beleaguered', *Yoga Journal* (July/August 1986).

Castaneda, Carlos, *The Teachings of Don Juan*, New York, Simon & Schuster, 1968.

Journey to Ixtlan, New York, Simon & Schuster, 1972.

A Separate Reality, New York, Simon & Schuster, 1972.

Dass, Ram and Steindl-Rast, David, 'An Encounter with Fritz Perls', in Jack Downing (ed.), *Gestalt Awareness*, New York, Perennial Library, Harper & Row, 1976.

'On Lay Monasticism', *Journal of Transpersonal Psychology*, 2 (1977).

Downing, George, *Massage Book*, New York, Random House, 1972.

Downing, Jack (ed.), *Gestalt Awareness*, New York, Perennial Library, Harper & Row, 1976.

Feynman, Richard P., Leighton, R. B., and Sands, M., *The Feynman Lectures on Physics*, Reading, Mass., Addison-Wesley, 1966.

Goldstein, Joseph, *The Experience of Insight: A Natural Unfolding*, Santa Cruz, University Press, 1976.

Goleman, D., *The Varieties of Religious Experience*, New York, Dutton, 1977.

'Buddhist and Western Psychology: Some Commonalities and Differences', *Journal of Transpersonal Psychology*, 13 (1981).

Hannah, Barbara, *Active Imagination*, Los Angeles, Sigo Press, 1981.

I Ching, see Wilhelm, Richard.

Inge, W. R., *Christian Mysticism,* New York, Meridian Books, 1956.

Iyengar, B. K. S., *Light on Yoga*, London, George Allen & Unwin Ltd, 1968.

Jung, C. G., *The Collected Works of C. G. Jung*, edited by Sir Herbert Read, Michael Fordham and Gerhard Adler, translated by R. F. C. Hull (except for Vol. 2), Princeton, New Jersey, Princeton University Press; and London, Routledge & Kegan Paul: Vol. 8, *The Structure and Dynamics of the Psyche*, 1960; Vol. 12, *Psychology and Alchemy*, 1944; Vol. 14, *Mysterium Coniunctionis: An Inquiry into the Separation and Synthesis of Psychic Opposites in Alchemy*, 1956; Vol. 16, *The Practice of Psychotherapy*, 1954.

Kalf, Dora, *Sand Play*, Boston, Sigo Press, 1981.

Kaplan, Amy, 'The Hidden Dance: An Introduction to Process-oriented Movement Work', Master's Thesis, Antioch University, Yellow Springs, Ohio, 1986.

Khanna, Madhu, *Yantra, Tantric Symbol of Cosmic Unity*, London, Thames & Hudson, 1979.

LeShan, Lawrence, *How to Meditate*, New York, Bantam Books, 1986.

Mann, Richard, *Light of Consciousness*, Albany, State University of New York, 1983.

Mindell, Arnold, *Dreambody*, Los Angeles, Sigo Press, 1982; and London, Routledge & Kegan Paul, 1984.

    Working with the Dreaming Body, London, Routledge & Kegan Paul, 1985.

    River's Way, London, Routledge & Kegan Paul, 1986.

    The Dreambody in Relationships, London, Routledge & Kegan Paul, 1987.

    City Shadows: Psychological Interventions in Psychiatry, London, Arkana, 1988.

    The Year 1, London, Arkana, 1989.

Coma, Key to Awakening, Boston, Shambhala, 1989.

The Year 1, Global Process Work with Planetary Tensions, London, Arkana, 1989.

Muktananda, Swami Baba, *The Play of Consciousness*, California, Shree Gurudev Siddha Yoga Ashram, 1974.

    See Peeth, Gurudev Siddha.

Patanjali, *The Yoga Sutras*, translated by Swami Prabhavananda and Christopher Isherwood, New York, Mentor, 1953.

Peeth, Gurudev Siddha, *In the Company of a Siddha. Interviews and Conversations with Swami Muktananda*, Ganeshpuri, India, 1981.

Perls, Fritz, *Gestalt Therapy Verbatim*, Lafayette, Real People Press, 1969.

Progoff, Ira, *The Practice of Process Meditation: The Intensive Journal Way to Spiritual Experience*, New York, Dialogue House Library, 1980.

Rawson, Philip, *Tantra: The Indian Cult of Ecstasy*, London, Thames & Hudson, 1973.

Reps, Paul (ed.), *Zen Flesh, Zen Bones*, New York, Anchor Books, 1961.

Rinpoche, Tarthang Tulku, 'A View of Mind', *Journal of Transpersonal Psychology*, 11 (1976).

Ruchpaul, Eva, *Hatha Yoga*, Paris, Presses Universitaires de France, 1978.

Satprem, *Sri Aurobindo or The Adventures of Consciousness*, New York, Harper & Row, 1974.

Sayadaw, Mahasi, *Practical Insight Meditation*, San Francisco, Unity Press, 1972.

Schultz, J. and Luthe, W., *Autogenic Training. A Psychophysiologic Approach in Psychotherapy*, New York, Grune & Stratton, 1955.

Shibayama, Z., *Zen Comments on the Mumoukan*, New York, Harper & Row, 1974.

Storm, H., *Seven Arrows*, New York, Harper & Row, 1972.

Suzuki, Shunryu, *Zen Mind, Beginner's Mind*, New York, Weatherhill, 1970.

Tart, Charles, *States of Consciousness, Psychological Processes*, El Cerito, California, Dutton, 1975.

'The Basic Nature of Altered States of Consciousness, A Systems Approach', *Journal of Transpersonal Psychology*, 1 (1976).

'Altered States of Consciousness and the Search for Enlightenment', *The Open Mind*, 2 (January 1985).

'Meditation', *The Open Mind*, 4 (Summer 1986).

Waking Up, Overcoming the Obstacles to Human Potential, Boston, Shambhala, 1987.

Thera, Nyanaponka, Satipatthana, *The Heart of Buddhist Meditation: A Handbook of Mental Training Based on the Buddha's Way of Mindfulness*, New York, Samuel Weiser, 1975.

Trungpa, Chogyam, *The Myth of Freedom*, Boston, Shambhala, 1976.

The Sacred Path of a Warrior, Boulder, Shambhala, 1984.

Underhill, Evelyn, *Mysticism: A Study in the Nature and Development of Man's Spiritual Consciousness*, New York, Dutton, 1911, 1961.

Washburn, M., 'Observations Relevant to a Unified Theory of Meditation', *Journal of Transpersonal Psychology*, 10 (1978).

Watts, Alan, *Psychotherapy East and West*, New York, Ballantine Books, 1968.

Weinhold, Barry and Beggs, James, *Transforming Persons and Programs*, Alexandria, Va., A.A.C.D. Press, 1984.

Whitehouse, Mary, 'C. G. Jung and Dance Therapy: Two Major Principles', in Penny Bernstein (ed.), *Eight Theoretical Approaches in Dance-Movement Therapy*, Dubuque, Iowa, Kendal/Hunt, 1979.

Wilbur, Ken, *The Atman Project: A Transpersonal View of Human Development*, Wheaton, Illinois, Theosophical Publishing House, 1982.

Wilhelm, Richard, *The I Ching or Book of Changes*, London, Routledge & Kegan Paul, 1973.

Worthington, Vivian, *A History of Yoga*, London, Routledge & Kegan Paul, 1982.

Bibliography

Wosien, Maria-Gabrielle, *The Sacred Dance: Encounter with the Gods*, New York, Avon, 1972.

Young, Shinzen, 'Stray Thoughts on Meditation', *The Open Mind*, 4 (Summer 1986).

Yu, Lu K'uan, *Taoist Yoga, Alchemy and Immortality*, London, Rider & Co., 1972.

Zimmer, H., *Philosophies of India*, London, Routledge & Kegan Paul, 1969.

INDEX

ARKANA – NEW-AGE BOOKS FOR MIND, BODY AND SPIRIT

With over 150 titles currently in print, Arkana is the leading name in quality new-age books for mind, body and spirit. Arkana encompasses the spirituality of both East and West, ancient and new, in fiction and non-fiction. A vast range of interests are covered, including Psychology and Transformation, Health, Science and Mysticism, Women's Spirituality and Astrology.

If you would like a catalogue of Arkana books, please write to:

Arkana Marketing Department
Penguin Books Ltd
27 Wright's Lane
London W8 5TZ

ARKANA – NEW-AGE BOOKS FOR MIND, BODY AND SPIRIT

A selection of titles already published or in preparation

Being Intimate: A Guide to Successful Relationships
John and Kris Amodeo

This invaluable guide aims to enrich one of the most important – yet often problematic – aspects of our lives: intimate relationships and friendships.

'A clear and practical guide to the realization and communication of authentic feelings, and thus an excellent pathway towards lasting intimacy and love' – George Leonard

The Brain Book Peter Russell

The essential handbook for brain users.

'A fascinating book – for everyone who is able to appreciate the human brain, which, as Russell says, is the most complex and most powerful information processor known to man. It is especially relevant for those who are called upon to read a great deal when time is limited, or who attend lectures or seminars and need to take notes' – *Nursing Times*

The Act of Creation Arthur Koestler

This second book in Koestler's classic trio of works on the human mind (which opened with *The Sleepwalkers* and concludes with *The Ghost in the Machine*) advances the theory that all creative activities – the conscious and unconscious processes underlying artistic orig-inality, scientific discovery and comic inspiration – share a basic pattern, which Koestler expounds and explores with all his usual clarity and brilliance.

A Psychology With a Soul: Psychosynthesis in Evolutionary Context Jean Hardy

Psychosynthesis was developed between 1910 and the 1950s by Roberto Assagioli – an Italian psychiatrist who, like Jung, diverged from Freud in search of a more spiritually based understanding of human nature. Jean Hardy's account of this comprehensive approach to self-realization will be of great value to everyone concerned with personal integration and spiritual growth.

ARKANA – NEW-AGE BOOKS FOR MIND, BODY AND SPIRIT

A selection of titles already published or in preparation

The TM Technique Peter Russell

Through a process precisely opposite to that by which the body accumulates stress and tension, transcendental meditation works to produce a state of profound rest, with positive benefits for health, clarity of mind, creativity and personal stability. Peter Russell's book has become the key work for everyone requiring a complete mastery of TM.

The Development of the Personality: Seminars in Psychological Astrology Volume I Liz Greene and Howard Sasportas

Taking as a starting point their groundbreaking work on the cross-fertilization between astrology and psychology, Liz Greene and Howard Sasportas show how depth psychology works with the natal chart to illuminate the experiences and problems all of us encounter throughout the development of our individual identity, from childhood onwards.

Homage to the Sun: The Wisdom of the Magus of Strovolos Kyriacos C. Markides

Homage to the Sun continues the adventure into the mysterious and extraordinary world of the spiritual teacher and healer Daskalos, the 'Magus of Strovolos'. The logical foundations of Daskalos' world of other dimensions are revealed to us – invisible masters, past-life memories and guardian angels, all explained by the Magus with great lucidity and scientific precision.

The Year I: Global Process Work Arnold Mindell

As we approach the end of the 20th century, we are on the verge of planetary extinction. Solving the planet's problems is literally a matter of life and death. Arnold Mindell shows how his famous and groundbreaking process-orientated psychology can be extended so that our own sense of global awareness can be developed and we – the whole community of earth's inhabitants – can comprehend the problems and work together towards solving them.